How to Get AARP Discounts on Kindle eBook

Steven Karson

Published by Steven Karson, 2024.

This is a work of fiction. Similarities to real people, places, or events are entirely coincidental.

HOW TO GET AARP DISCOUNTS ON KINDLE EBOOK

First edition. June 19, 2024.

Copyright © 2024 Steven Karson.

Written by Steven Karson.

Table of Contents

Chapter 1 1

Chapter 2 11

Chapter 3 31

Chapter 4 41

Chapter 5 53

Chapter 6 61

Chapter 7 71

Chapter 8 81

Chapter 9 93

Chapter 1

Introduction

AARP Membership and Kindle eBooks

For many, curling up with a captivating Kindle eBook offers a delightful escape into new worlds and cherished knowledge. But did you know that your AARP membership can unlock a treasure trove of savings on these digital reads? This guide delves into the exciting synergy between AARP and Kindle, empowering you to maximize your reading enjoyment while stretching your budget further.

Understanding AARP Membership Benefits:

The American Association of Retired Persons (AARP) champions the well-being of individuals aged 50 and above. Beyond valuable resources and advocacy, AARP membership unlocks a world of exclusive discounts, including those on Kindle eBooks. These savings can range from enticing percentage reductions to fixed-amount markdowns, making your favorite titles even more affordable.

A Seamless Blend: AARP and the Kindle Ecosystem:

Whether you're a seasoned Kindle aficionado or a curious newcomer, the good news is that integrating AARP discounts into your reading experience is refreshingly straightforward. Here's a breakdown of how AARP and Kindle beautifully complement each other:

Eligibility: If you're an AARP member, you're already well on your way to enjoying discounted Kindle eBooks. No additional enrollment or complicated procedures are necessary.

Finding Discounted Titles: Amazon, the parent company of Kindle, offers a dedicated section for AARP-discounted eBooks. Here, you'll find a curated selection of titles across a variety of genres, ensuring there's something for every reader's taste.

Discount Recognition: Identifying AARP-discounted eBooks is a breeze. Look for the AARP discount badge displayed prominently on the book's detail page. Additionally, some titles might explicitly mention the AARP discount in their descriptions.

Beyond the AARP Section: Expanding Your Savings Horizons:

While the AARP section on Amazon is a fantastic starting point, your discount-finding journey doesn't have to end there. Here are some additional strategies to unearth even more savings:

Advanced Search Techniques: The powerful search functionality on Amazon allows you to leverage your AARP membership. Include search terms like "AARP discount" or "AARP member deal" alongside your desired genre or author to uncover hidden gems.

AARP's Resource Arsenal: The AARP website often features curated lists or recommendations for AARP-discounted Kindle eBooks. These lists can be categorized by genre, theme, or even special occasions, making it simple to find the perfect discounted read for any mood.

Staying Updated: To ensure you never miss out on the latest AARP Kindle deals, consider subscribing to AARP's email alerts or following their social media accounts. AARP regularly broadcasts information about ongoing discounts and exclusive offers on eBooks.

Maximizing Your Savings Potential:

Here are some additional tips to maximize your AARP Kindle savings:

Compare Prices: While the AARP discount is a fantastic benefit, it's always wise to compare prices with other retailers, particularly for older titles. You might occasionally find a better deal elsewhere.

Free eBook Options: Don't forget about the plethora of free eBooks available on Kindle. AARP itself curates a selection of free downloadable eBooks for its members. Additionally, many publishers offer free samples or first chapters of their titles, allowing you to try before you buy.

Kindle Unlimited: If you're a voracious reader, consider exploring Kindle Unlimited, a subscription service offering unlimited access to a vast library of eBooks for a monthly fee. While not directly related to AARP discounts, Kindle Unlimited can be a cost-effective option for those who read frequently.

By leveraging your AARP membership and the vast Kindle ecosystem, you can embark on a rewarding journey of affordable literary exploration. With a little savvy searching and strategic planning, you can unlock a world of discounted eBooks, keeping your reading list brimming without breaking the bank. So, grab your favorite Kindle device, dive into the treasure trove of AARP discounts, and get ready to lose yourself in the captivating world of discounted eBooks!

Benefits of AARP Membership

While discounted Kindle eBooks are a delightful perk of AARP membership, the benefits extend far beyond the digital bookshelf. AARP membership unlocks a treasure trove of advantages designed to empower individuals aged 50 and above to live life to the fullest. Let's delve into the diverse and enriching benefits that come with being an AARP member.

Financial Security and Savings:

Discounts Galore: AARP membership opens doors to a world of discounts across various sectors. From travel and healthcare to entertainment and everyday purchases, members enjoy significant savings on a wide range of products and services. Imagine securing better rates on car insurance, snagging exclusive deals on groceries, or enjoying discounts on your next home improvement project – all thanks to your AARP membership.

Investment and Retirement Planning: AARP offers valuable resources and guidance on navigating the complexities of financial planning. Whether you're nearing retirement or seeking to optimize your existing investments, AARP provides access to educational materials, workshops, and consultations with financial experts. This can be especially helpful as you transition into retirement and need to make informed decisions about your nest egg.

Insurance Solutions: AARP negotiates competitive rates and plans with leading insurance providers, offering members access to affordable health, dental, vision, and life insurance options. This can provide peace of mind and significant cost savings on essential coverage. Imagine finding a health insurance plan that caters to your specific needs at a price you can afford, or securing a life insurance policy that protects your loved ones without breaking the bank.

Health and Wellness:

Health Advocacy: AARP is a strong advocate for policies and initiatives that promote the health and well-being of older adults. They actively lobby for improved access to healthcare, affordable medications, and preventative care services. This advocacy ensures that your voice is heard when it comes to shaping policies that affect your health and well-being.

Wellness Resources: AARP offers a wealth of information and resources on maintaining a healthy lifestyle. This includes educational materials on healthy eating, fitness tips, chronic disease management strategies, and mental well-being tools. You'll find practical advice on everything from incorporating exercise into your daily routine to managing chronic conditions like diabetes or arthritis.

Discounts on Health and Fitness Products: AARP membership unlocks discounts on various health and fitness products and services. This can range from gym memberships and fitness trackers to discounts on hearing aids, eyeglasses, and other health essentials. Imagine getting a discount on the latest fitness tracker to help you stay motivated, or finding affordable hearing aids that improve your quality of life.

Travel and Leisure:

Travel Deals and Discounts: AARP members enjoy exclusive discounts on hotels, cruises, tours, car rentals, and other travel-related expenses. This allows them to explore the world and experience new cultures at a more affordable price. Imagine booking your dream vacation to Italy for less, or finding a discounted cruise that lets you explore the wonders of the Caribbean without breaking the bank.

Travel Planning Assistance: AARP offers travel planning resources and assistance to help members plan their dream vacations. This includes curated travel itineraries, destination guides, and recommendations for senior-friendly travel options. Whether you're looking for a relaxing beach getaway or an adventurous hiking trip, AARP can help you plan a safe and enjoyable vacation tailored to your interests and abilities.

Volunteer Opportunities: AARP connects members with various volunteer opportunities. This allows individuals to stay active and engaged in their communities while making a positive impact on the lives of others. Imagine using your skills and experience to mentor young people, volunteer at a local hospital, or help protect the environment – all while staying connected to your community.

Social Connection and Lifelong Learning:

Community Events and Activities: AARP organizes and promotes local events and activities designed for the 50+ age group. These events offer opportunities for social interaction, learning new skills, and fostering a sense of belonging. Imagine attending a local lecture on healthy aging, participating in a book club discussion, or joining a group fitness class – all opportunities to connect with like-minded individuals and build new friendships.

Lifelong Learning Resources: AARP champions lifelong learning and provides access to educational resources and programs designed for older adults. This includes online courses, lectures, workshops, and book clubs that cater to a wide range of interests. Imagine taking an online course on photography, attending a lecture on the history of jazz music, or joining a book club that discusses classic novels – all ways to keep your mind sharp and explore new interests.

Grandparenting Support: AARP offers resources and support for grandparents, providing valuable advice on navigating the joys and challenges of grandparenting in today's world. Imagine finding tips on how to communicate effectively with your grandchildren, learning about the latest trends in child development, or connecting with other grandparents to share experiences and support.

Technology Assistance:

Tech Education Workshops: AARP recognizes the importance of technology in today's world and offers educational workshops and resources to help members stay tech-savvy. This can include learning basic computer skills, using social media platforms, navigating online banking systems, or troubleshooting common tech issues. Imagine attending a workshop on mastering your smartphone camera, learning how to stay safe online, or getting comfortable with video conferencing tools – all ways to embrace technology and stay connected with loved ones.

Discounts on Technology Products and Services: AARP negotiates discounts with leading technology companies, allowing members to purchase computers, tablets, internet access plans, and other technology-related products and services at more affordable prices. Imagine getting a discount on a new laptop to connect with friends and family virtually, or finding affordable internet access that allows you to stay connected to the world.

Member Magazine and Online Community:

AARP The Magazine: AARP membership includes a subscription to AARP The Magazine, a trusted publication featuring articles on health, wellness, finances, travel, and other topics relevant to the 50+ age group. Imagine receiving a monthly magazine filled with informative articles, inspiring stories, and practical advice tailored to your lifestyle.

Online Community Platform: AARP offers a vibrant online community platform where members can connect with each other, share experiences, discuss topics of interest, and participate in online forums. This allows you to build a network of like-minded individuals, ask questions, and offer support to others. Imagine joining a forum to discuss healthy recipes, participate in an online discussion about a new book, or connect with others who share your passion for travel – all within the AARP online community.

AARP membership is more than just a gateway to discounted Kindle eBooks. It's a comprehensive package designed to empower individuals aged 50 and above to live fulfilling and enriching lives. From financial security and health resources to travel opportunities and social connections, AARP offers a wealth of benefits that cater to various aspects of your life. By leveraging these benefits, you can navigate the exciting journey of aging with confidence, knowledge, and a sense of community. So, whether you're seeking to optimize your finances, prioritize your health, explore the world, or connect with others, AARP membership can be a valuable companion on your path to a vibrant and fulfilling second act.

Introduction to Kindle Devices and Apps

For those new to the world of Kindle, understanding the different devices and apps available can feel overwhelming. But fret not! This section serves as your friendly guide, demystifying the Kindle ecosystem and empowering you to seamlessly navigate your journey towards discounted eBooks.

The Kindle Device Family: A Spectrum of Reading Options

Kindle devices come in various shapes and sizes, catering to diverse reading preferences and budgets. Here's a breakdown of the most popular Kindle devices:

Kindle (Basic): This compact and lightweight e-reader offers a no-frills reading experience, perfect for those who prioritize portability and affordability. It boasts a glare-free display optimized for reading even in bright sunlight, and a long battery life that allows you to enjoy days (or even weeks) of reading on a single charge.

Kindle Paperwhite: This mid-range option elevates the reading experience with a built-in adjustable front light, ideal for reading in low-light conditions. It also features a sharper display resolution compared to the basic Kindle, offering crisper text and enhanced visuals for images and diagrams.

Kindle Oasis: For the ultimate in reading comfort and luxury, the Kindle Oasis reigns supreme. This sleek and ergonomic device boasts a larger display with adjustable warm lighting, perfect for extended reading sessions. Additionally, the Oasis features physical page turn buttons, catering to those who prefer a more traditional book-like feel.

Beyond Devices: The Power of Kindle Apps

While Kindle devices offer a dedicated e-reading experience, the Kindle ecosystem extends beyond physical hardware. Here's where the versatility of Kindle apps comes into play:

Free Kindle App for Smartphones and Tablets: Turn your existing smartphone or tablet into a powerful eBook reader with the free Kindle app. Available for iOS, Android, Windows, and Mac, the app allows you to access your Kindle library, purchase new eBooks, and seamlessly sync your reading progress across all your devices. This means you can start reading a book on your phone during your commute and pick up right where you left off on your Kindle device later.

Kindle App for Computers: For those who prefer reading on a larger screen, the Kindle app is also available for computers. This allows you to download and read eBooks on your PC or Mac, making your Kindle library accessible from virtually any device.

Common Features Across the Kindle Ecosystem:

Regardless of the device or app you choose, the core Kindle experience offers several key features that enhance your reading enjoyment:

Vast eBook Library: The Kindle Store boasts millions of eBooks across a wide range of genres, from fiction and non-fiction to classics and contemporary bestsellers. With such a vast selection, you're sure to find something that piques your interest, all at your fingertips.

Whispersync Technology: This innovative feature seamlessly synchronizes your reading progress, bookmarks, notes, and highlights across all your Kindle devices and apps. This allows you to switch between devices without losing your place or annotations. Imagine starting a book on your phone during your lunch break, then continuing seamlessly on your Kindle device later that evening – all thanks to Whispersync.

Customization Options: Tailor your reading experience to your preferences. Adjust font size, style, and text alignment to optimize comfort and readability. Additionally, many Kindle devices and apps offer adjustable lighting settings, allowing you to find the perfect level of brightness for any environment.

Built-in Dictionary and Word Lookup: Encounter an unfamiliar word while reading? No problem! Kindle devices and apps come with built-in dictionaries, allowing you to instantly look up definitions and enhance your vocabulary.

Choosing the Right Kindle Device or App:

The ideal choice depends on your individual needs and preferences. Consider these factors when making your decision:

Reading Habits: Do you primarily read on the go? Then a lightweight and portable device like the Kindle (Basic) might be ideal. If you prefer reading for extended periods at home, a larger device like the Kindle Paperwhite or Oasis might be more comfortable.

Budget: Kindle devices range in price, with the basic model being the most affordable option. Consider your budget and prioritize features that are most important to you.

Device Compatibility: Ensure the Kindle app is compatible with your existing smartphone, tablet, or computer.

The Kindle ecosystem offers a diverse range of devices and apps, catering to various reading styles and preferences. Understanding these options empowers you to choose the ideal platform for enjoying discounted Kindle eBooks. From the portability of the Kindle (Basic) to the immersive experience of the Kindle Oasis, the possibilities are endless. So, dive into the world of Kindle, explore the vast library of discounted eBooks, and embark on a captivating reading journey tailored to your unique needs.

Chapter 2

Joining AARP (Optional for Existing Members)

Embracing the AARP Advantage: Joining and Verifying Your Membership

For those who haven't already embarked on their AARP journey, this section delves into the simple process of joining and unlocking the world of benefits, including, of course, the exciting prospect of discounted Kindle eBooks. Even existing members might find valuable information here, particularly regarding membership verification, a crucial step when claiming AARP discounts on Kindle.

Eligibility for AARP Membership:

AARP membership is open to individuals aged 50 and above. There are no additional requirements or prerequisites. Whether you're actively employed, nearing retirement, or already enjoying your golden years, AARP membership can enrich your life in countless ways.

Joining AARP: A Streamlined Process

Joining AARP is a breeze. Here are the two convenient methods at your disposal:

- **Online Enrollment:** Visit the AARP website (https://www.aarp.org/) and navigate to the membership section. Follow the on-screen prompts, providing basic information such as your name, date of birth, contact details, and preferred membership option. The online enrollment process is straightforward and secure, allowing you to become an AARP member within minutes.
- **Telephone Enrollment:** If you prefer a more personal touch, AARP offers a dedicated phone line for membership inquiries. Call the toll-free number (1-888-OUR-AARP; 1-888-687-2277) and speak with

a friendly AARP representative who will guide you through the enrollment process.

Membership Options and Costs:

AARP offers various membership options to suit your needs and budget. Here's a breakdown of the most common choices:

- **Individual Membership:** This is the basic membership plan, offering access to all core AARP benefits, including discounts, resources, and the AARP magazine.
- **Dual Membership:** This plan extends benefits to both you and your spouse or partner residing in the same household.
- **Multi-Year Memberships:** AARP offers discounted rates for enrolling in multi-year memberships. This is a cost-effective option for those who plan to stay with AARP for several years.

Payment Options:

AARP accepts various payment methods for your membership, including credit cards, debit cards, and electronic checks. Choose the option that aligns best with your financial preferences.

Welcome to the AARP Family!

Congratulations, you're now an AARP member! You'll receive a welcome packet containing your membership card, information about accessing online resources, and details on maximizing your AARP benefits.

Existing AARP Members: Verifying Your Membership for Kindle Discounts

Even if you're already an AARP member, an important step remains when it comes to claiming AARP discounts on Kindle eBooks: verifying your membership with Amazon. This allows Amazon to confirm your eligibility and apply the corresponding discounts at checkout.

HOW TO GET AARP DISCOUNTS ON KINDLE EBOOK

Here's how to verify your AARP membership on Amazon:

- **Navigate to Your Account Settings:** Log in to your Amazon account and navigate to "Your Account" settings. Here, you'll find various options related to your account information and preferences.
- **Locate the "Manage Your AARP Membership" Section:** Within your account settings, look for a section titled "Manage Your AARP Membership" or similar wording. This section allows you to link your AARP membership to your Amazon account.
- **Enter Your Membership Information:** Carefully enter your AARP membership number and any other required details in the designated fields.
- **Verification Process:** Once you enter your information, Amazon will initiate a verification process with AARP to confirm your membership status. This process typically takes a few minutes to complete.
- **Confirmation and AARP Benefits:** Upon successful verification, your AARP membership will be linked to your Amazon account. This unlocks your access to AARP discounts on Kindle eBooks and other eligible products on the Amazon platform.

Troubleshooting Membership Verification Issues:

If you encounter any difficulties during the verification process, here are some troubleshooting tips:

- **Double-check your information:** Ensure you've entered your AARP membership number accurately, including any hyphens or spaces.
- **Contact AARP or Amazon Customer Support:** For assistance with membership verification or any other inquiries, don't hesitate to contact either AARP or Amazon customer support. Both organizations offer dedicated phone lines and online support platforms to address your concerns.

Joining AARP opens a treasure chest of benefits, and the verification process ensures you can fully embrace these advantages, particularly when seeking discounted Kindle eBooks. With your AARP membership linked to your Amazon account, you're ready to embark on a rewarding journey of affordable literary exploration. So, join the AARP community, verify your membership, and delve into a world of discounted Kindle eBooks, waiting to be discovered!

Eligibility Requirements

The prospect of discounted Kindle eBooks is undoubtedly enticing. But before diving headfirst into this world of literary savings, it's crucial to understand the eligibility requirements for AARP membership. This section clarifies who can join AARP and, consequently, unlock the door to discounted eBooks on your Kindle device.

Age Requirement: The Gateway to AARP Benefits

The cornerstone of AARP eligibility revolves around age. AARP membership is open to individuals aged 50 and above. There's no strict birthday cutoff; as long as you turn 50 in the current year, you qualify for membership. This straightforward age requirement ensures that individuals entering a new life stage – often characterized by retirement planning, financial considerations, and a focus on well-being – can access valuable resources and support, including discounted Kindle eBooks.

Beyond Age: Considerations for Spouses and Partners

While the primary membership is based on individual eligibility, AARP caters to households as well. Here's what you need to know:

- **Dual Membership:** If you're married or in a committed partnership residing in the same household, you can opt for a dual membership. This extends all the benefits of AARP membership to both partners, including access to discounted Kindle eBooks. This option is particularly cost-effective for couples who both enjoy reading and want to maximize their savings on eBooks.

- **Household Sharing:** Even with individual memberships, AARP allows a secondary membership for a spouse or partner within the same household. This secondary membership doesn't carry the full benefits of a primary membership but often includes access to discounted Kindle eBooks and other select AARP benefits.

Understanding Exceptions and Special Cases:

While the age requirement is the primary criterion, AARP acknowledges that life isn't always straightforward. Here are some additional points to consider:

- **Early Retirement:** If you've retired early, before the age of 50, you might still be eligible for AARP membership under special circumstances. AARP offers membership to certain professions with a high retirement rate, such as law enforcement officers and firefighters. It's always best to check the AARP website or contact customer support to inquire about eligibility in such cases.
- **Disability Benefits:** Individuals receiving Social Security Disability Insurance (SSDI) benefits may be eligible for AARP membership before the age of 50. Again, it's recommended to verify eligibility directly with AARP to ensure you meet the specific criteria.

No Geographic Restrictions: Unleashing Savings Worldwide

The beauty of AARP membership lies in its universality. As long as you meet the age requirement or qualify under one of the special exceptions, you can enjoy AARP benefits, including discounted Kindle eBooks, regardless of your location. Whether you reside in the United States, Canada, or another country worldwide, you can leverage your AARP membership to unlock a world of affordable reading experiences on your Kindle device.

Membership Verification: The Final Hurdle

Even after confirming your eligibility, there's one crucial step before claiming your AARP discounts on Kindle eBooks: verifying your membership with Amazon. This process involves linking your AARP membership number to your Amazon account, allowing the platform to confirm your eligibility and apply the corresponding discounts at checkout. The verification process is typically straightforward, and our guide will walk you through it step-by-step in a later section.

Understanding AARP's eligibility requirements is the first step towards unlocking a universe of discounted Kindle eBooks. By meeting the age requirement (or qualifying under a special exception) and following the straightforward verification process, you'll be well on your way to enriching your reading life with significant savings. So, if you're 50 or above (or meet specific exceptions), embrace the world of AARP membership and explore a treasure trove of discounted Kindle eBooks waiting to be discovered.

Membership Options and Costs:

AARP membership unlocks a treasure trove of benefits, but when it comes to discounted Kindle eBooks, understanding the various membership options and associated costs becomes crucial. This section delves into the different membership plans offered by AARP, empowering you to select the option that aligns best with your needs and budget, ultimately maximizing your savings on eBooks.

Individual Membership: The Foundation for Savings

This is the most basic and widely chosen AARP membership option. It grants you access to the core benefits offered by AARP, including:

- **Discounted Kindle eBooks:** This is the key benefit explored in this book, allowing you to unlock significant savings on a vast library of eBooks through Amazon.
- **AARP The Magazine:** A monthly subscription to AARP The Magazine, featuring informative articles on health, finances, travel, and other topics relevant to the 50+ age group.
- **Discounts on Travel, Healthcare, and Everyday Purchases:** AARP negotiates discounts with various companies, offering members savings on travel, healthcare products and services, entertainment, and everyday purchases.
- **Access to Online Resources and Tools:** The AARP website offers a wealth of information, resources, and tools designed to support individuals aged 50 and above.
- **Eligibility for AARP Events and Activities:** AARP organizes local events and activities catering to the interests and needs of the 50+ population.

The individual membership is a cost-effective entry point for those seeking to explore the benefits of AARP, including discounted Kindle eBooks.

Dual Membership: Extending Savings to Your Household

If you're married or in a committed partnership residing in the same household, the dual membership option is an excellent choice. It grants all the benefits of an individual membership to both partners, essentially doubling the value you receive from your AARP membership. This translates to:

- **Two AARP Cards:** Both partners receive separate AARP membership cards, allowing them to claim individual discounts and access benefits independently.
- **Double the Discounted Kindle eBooks:** Both partners can enjoy AARP discounts on Kindle eBooks, expanding your collective savings on digital reading materials.
- **Shared Access to Online Resources and Tools:** Both partners gain access to AARP's online resources and tools, allowing you to explore information and utilize benefits together.

The dual membership is ideal for couples who want to maximize their savings on AARP benefits, including discounted Kindle eBooks, while sharing access to other valuable resources.

Exploring Cost Considerations: Making an Informed Decision

Here's a breakdown of the pricing structure for individual and dual memberships:

- **Individual Membership:** AARP offers various payment options for individual memberships. The most common pricing models include:
    - **Yearly Membership:** This is the most cost-effective option in the long run. You'll typically pay a lower price per month compared to monthly or short-term plans.
    - **Monthly Membership:** This option provides flexibility for those who prefer to pay on a monthly basis. However, the cost per month is usually higher than a yearly membership.
    - **Short-Term Memberships:** AARP might offer introductory or promotional offers with short-term memberships at discounted rates. However, these often require renewal at a higher price after the initial

HOW TO GET AARP DISCOUNTS ON KINDLE EBOOK

period.
- **Dual Membership:** Dual memberships typically cost slightly more than individual memberships, reflecting the extended benefits for two partners. The pricing structure often mirrors the individual membership options, with yearly payments offering the best cost savings overall.

Additional Factors to Consider When Choosing a Membership:

Beyond the core benefits mentioned earlier, some additional factors might influence your choice:

- **Frequency of eBook Reading:** If you're an avid reader who regularly purchases Kindle eBooks, the cost savings accrued through AARP discounts can significantly outweigh the membership fee.
- **Planned Use of Other AARP Benefits:** Do you anticipate utilizing other AARP benefits, such as travel discounts or online resources? If so, the value proposition of a membership increases.
- **Budgetary Constraints:** Carefully consider your budget and choose the membership option that aligns best with your financial limitations.

Multi-Year Memberships: Saving More with Long-Term Commitment

For those who plan to stay with AARP for several years, multi-year membership options can offer significant savings. These plans typically lock in a lower price per year compared to annual renewals. However, they require a longer upfront commitment. Carefully assess your long-term plans before opting for a multi-year membership.

Exploring Free Trials and Introductory Offers

AARP occasionally offers free trials or introductory memberships at discounted rates. This can be a fantastic way to explore the AARP experience, including discounted Kindle eBooks, before committing to a full membership.

Eligibility Requirements

Unlocking Savings: Understanding AARP Membership Eligibility for Kindle Discounts

The prospect of discounted Kindle eBooks is undoubtedly enticing. But before diving headfirst into this world of literary savings, it's crucial to understand the eligibility requirements for AARP membership. This section clarifies who can join AARP and, consequently, unlock the door to discounted eBooks on your Kindle device.

Age Requirement: The Gateway to AARP Benefits

The cornerstone of AARP eligibility revolves around age. AARP membership is open to individuals aged 50 and above. There's no strict birthday cutoff; as long as you turn 50 in the current year, you qualify for membership. This straightforward age requirement ensures that individuals entering a new life stage – often characterized by retirement planning, financial considerations, and a focus on well-being – can access valuable resources and support, including discounted Kindle eBooks.

Beyond Age: Considerations for Spouses and Partners

While the primary membership is based on individual eligibility, AARP caters to households as well. Here's what you need to know:

Dual Membership: If you're married or in a committed partnership residing in the same household, you can opt for a dual membership. This extends all the benefits of AARP membership to both partners, including access to discounted Kindle eBooks. This option is particularly cost-effective for couples who both enjoy reading and want to maximize their savings on eBooks.

Household Sharing: Even with individual memberships, AARP allows a secondary membership for a spouse or partner within the same household. This secondary membership doesn't carry the full benefits of a primary membership but often includes access to discounted Kindle eBooks and other select AARP benefits.

Understanding Exceptions and Special Cases:

While the age requirement is the primary criterion, AARP acknowledges that life isn't always straightforward. Here are some additional points to consider:

Early Retirement: If you've retired early, before the age of 50, you might still be eligible for AARP membership under special circumstances. AARP offers membership to certain professions with a high retirement rate, such as law enforcement officers and firefighters. It's always best to check the AARP website or contact customer support to inquire about eligibility in such cases.

Disability Benefits: Individuals receiving Social Security Disability Insurance (SSDI) benefits may be eligible for AARP membership before the age of 50. Again, it's recommended to verify eligibility directly with AARP to ensure you meet the specific criteria.

No Geographic Restrictions: Unleashing Savings Worldwide

The beauty of AARP membership lies in its universality. As long as you meet the age requirement or qualify under one of the special exceptions, you can enjoy AARP benefits, including discounted Kindle eBooks, regardless of your location. Whether you reside in the United States, Canada, or another country worldwide, you can leverage your AARP membership to unlock a world of affordable reading experiences on your Kindle device.

Membership Verification: The Final Hurdle

Even after confirming your eligibility, there's one crucial step before claiming your AARP discounts on Kindle eBooks: verifying your membership with Amazon. This process involves linking your AARP membership number to your Amazon account, allowing the platform to confirm your eligibility and apply the corresponding discounts at checkout. The verification process is typically straightforward, and our guide will walk you through it step-by-step in a later section.

Understanding AARP's eligibility requirements is the first step towards unlocking a universe of discounted Kindle eBooks. By meeting the age requirement (or qualifying under a special exception) and following the straightforward verification process, you'll be well on your way to enriching your reading life with significant savings. So, if you're 50 or above (or meet specific exceptions), embrace the world of AARP membership and explore a treasure trove of discounted Kindle eBooks waiting to be discovered.

Membership Options and Costs

Decoding AARP Membership Options: Choosing the Perfect Fit for Discounted eBooks

AARP membership unlocks a treasure trove of benefits, but when it comes to discounted Kindle eBooks, understanding the various membership options and associated costs becomes crucial. This section delves into the different membership plans offered by AARP, empowering you to select the option that aligns best with your needs and budget, ultimately maximizing your savings on eBooks.

Individual Membership: The Foundation for Savings

This is the most basic and widely chosen AARP membership option. It grants you access to the core benefits offered by AARP, including:

Discounted Kindle eBooks: This is the key benefit explored in this book, allowing you to unlock significant savings on a vast library of eBooks through Amazon.

AARP The Magazine: A monthly subscription to AARP The Magazine, featuring informative articles on health, finances, travel, and other topics relevant to the 50+ age group.

Discounts on Travel, Healthcare, and Everyday Purchases: AARP negotiates discounts with various companies, offering members savings on travel, healthcare products and services, entertainment, and everyday purchases.

Access to Online Resources and Tools: The AARP website offers a wealth of information, resources, and tools designed to support individuals aged 50 and above.

Eligibility for AARP Events and Activities: AARP organizes local events and activities catering to the interests and needs of the 50+ population.

The individual membership is a cost-effective entry point for those seeking to explore the benefits of AARP, including discounted Kindle eBooks.

Dual Membership: Extending Savings to Your Household

If you're married or in a committed partnership residing in the same household, the dual membership option is an excellent choice. It grants all the benefits of an individual membership to both partners, essentially doubling the value you receive from your AARP membership. This translates to:

Two AARP Cards: Both partners receive separate AARP membership cards, allowing them to claim individual discounts and access benefits independently.

Double the Discounted Kindle eBooks: Both partners can enjoy AARP discounts on Kindle eBooks, expanding your collective savings on digital reading materials.

Shared Access to Online Resources and Tools: Both partners gain access to AARP's online resources and tools, allowing you to explore information and utilize benefits together.

The dual membership is ideal for couples who want to maximize their savings on AARP benefits, including discounted Kindle eBooks, while sharing access to other valuable resources.

Exploring Cost Considerations: Making an Informed Decision

Here's a breakdown of the pricing structure for individual and dual memberships:

Individual Membership: AARP offers various payment options for individual memberships. The most common pricing models include:

Yearly Membership: This is the most cost-effective option in the long run. You'll typically pay a lower price per month compared to monthly or short-term plans.

Monthly Membership: This option provides flexibility for those who prefer to pay on a monthly basis. However, the cost per month is usually higher than a yearly membership.

Short-Term Memberships: AARP might offer introductory or promotional offers with short-term memberships at discounted rates. However, these often require renewal at a higher price after the initial period.

Dual Membership: Dual memberships typically cost slightly more than individual memberships, reflecting the extended benefits for two partners. The pricing structure often mirrors the individual membership options, with yearly payments offering the best cost savings overall.

Additional Factors to Consider When Choosing a Membership:

Beyond the core benefits mentioned earlier, some additional factors might influence your choice:

Frequency of eBook Reading: If you're an avid reader who regularly purchases Kindle eBooks, the cost savings accrued through AARP discounts can significantly outweigh the membership fee.

Planned Use of Other AARP Benefits: Do you anticipate utilizing other AARP benefits, such as travel discounts or online resources? If so, the value proposition of a membership increases.

Budgetary Constraints: Carefully consider your budget and choose the membership option that aligns best with your financial limitations.

Multi-Year Memberships: Saving More with Long-Term Commitment

For those who plan to stay with AARP for several years, multi-year membership options can offer significant savings. These plans typically lock in a lower price per year compared to annual renewals. However, they require a longer upfront commitment. Carefully assess your long-term plans before opting for a multi-year membership.

Exploring Free Trials and Introductory Offers

AARP occasionally offers free trials or introductory memberships at discounted rates. This can be a fantastic way to explore the AARP experience, including discounted Kindle eBooks, before committing to a full membership.

The Crucial Step: Verifying Your AARP Membership for Discounted eBooks

Having an AARP membership unlocks a treasure trove of benefits, including the exciting prospect of discounted Kindle eBooks. But before diving headfirst into this world of literary savings, a crucial step remains: verifying your membership with Amazon. This section guides you through the simple process of linking your AARP membership to your Amazon account, ensuring you can seamlessly claim those coveted discounts on your next Kindle purchase.

Why Verification is Essential

While having an AARP membership grants access to various benefits, verification with Amazon is crucial specifically for claiming discounted Kindle eBooks. This verification process allows Amazon to confirm your eligibility for AARP discounts and apply them automatically at checkout. Without verification, you might miss out on these significant savings when purchasing eBooks on your Kindle device.

Verifying Your Membership: A Smooth Process

The verification process is straightforward and can be completed in a few minutes. Here's a detailed breakdown of the steps involved:

Navigate to Your Account Settings: The first step is to access your Amazon account settings. Log in to your Amazon account and locate the "Your Account" section. This section typically houses various options related to your account information and preferences. Look for options like "Account," "Your Account," or "Manage Your Account," depending on the specific layout of the Amazon website.

Finding the AARP Verification Section: Once you're within your account settings, locate the section dedicated to verifying your AARP membership. This might be titled "Manage Your AARP Membership," "AARP Discounts," or something similar. If you have difficulty finding the exact section, utilize the search function within your account settings to locate "AARP" or "Membership Verification."

Entering Your Membership Information: Once you've identified the correct section, you'll be prompted to enter your AARP membership information. This typically involves providing your AARP membership number. Ensure you enter the number accurately, including any hyphens or spaces present in your membership card. Double-check the information before proceeding to avoid any verification delays.

Initiating the Verification Process: After entering your membership number, click the button to initiate the verification process. Amazon will then communicate with AARP to confirm the validity of your membership number and your eligibility for AARP discounts.

Confirmation and AARP Benefits: Upon successful verification, a confirmation message will appear on your screen. You'll receive a notification confirming that your AARP membership is now linked to your Amazon account. This unlocks your access to discounted Kindle eBooks and potentially other AARP benefits available on the Amazon platform, depending on your membership level.

Troubleshooting Verification Issues: Solutions at Your Fingertips

In rare instances, you might encounter issues during the verification process. Here's how to troubleshoot common problems:

Double-check Information: The most frequent stumbling block is inaccurate information entry. Ensure you've entered your AARP membership number precisely, including any hyphens or spaces. A single typo can cause verification failure.

Check Membership Status: If entering the information correctly doesn't resolve the issue, verify that your AARP membership is active and in good standing. You can check your membership status by logging into the AARP website or contacting AARP customer support.

Contact Customer Support: For any persistent verification issues, don't hesitate to reach out to either AARP or Amazon customer support. Both organizations offer dedicated phone lines and online support platforms to address your concerns.

Additional Tips for a Smooth Verification Process:

Maintain Updated Information: Ensure your AARP membership information, including your email address and contact details, is up-to-date on both the AARP website and your Amazon account. This facilitates smooth communication during the verification process.

Consider Multi-Factor Authentication: For enhanced security, consider enabling multi-factor authentication (MFA) on both your AARP and Amazon accounts. This adds an extra layer of protection and can potentially prevent any unauthorized attempts to link your accounts.

Beyond Verification: Ongoing Benefits

Once you've successfully verified your AARP membership, you're ready to explore a world of discounted Kindle eBooks. Remember to keep your AARP membership active to maintain access to these savings and continue enjoying the plethora of benefits offered by AARP.

Verifying Your AARP Membership

Having an AARP membership unlocks a treasure trove of benefits, including the exciting prospect of discounted Kindle eBooks. But before diving headfirst into this world of literary savings, a crucial step remains: verifying your membership with Amazon. This section guides you through the simple process of linking your AARP membership to your Amazon account, ensuring you can seamlessly claim those coveted discounts on your next Kindle purchase.

Why Verification is Essential

While having an AARP membership grants access to various benefits, verification with Amazon is crucial specifically for claiming discounted Kindle eBooks. This verification process allows Amazon to confirm your eligibility for AARP discounts and apply them automatically at checkout. Without verification, you might miss out on these significant savings when purchasing eBooks on your Kindle device.

Verifying Your Membership: A Smooth Process

The verification process is straightforward and can be completed in a few minutes. Here's a detailed breakdown of the steps involved:

1. **Navigate to Your Account Settings:** The first step is to access your Amazon account settings. Log in to your Amazon account and locate the "Your Account" section. This section typically houses various options related to your account information and preferences. Look for options like "Account," "Your Account," or "Manage Your Account," depending on the specific layout of the Amazon website.
2. **Finding the AARP Verification Section:** Once you're within your account settings, locate the section dedicated to verifying your AARP membership. This might be titled "Manage Your AARP Membership," "AARP Discounts," or something similar. If you have difficulty finding the exact section, utilize the search function within your account settings to locate "AARP" or "Membership Verification."
3. **Entering Your Membership Information:** Once you've identified the correct section, you'll be prompted to enter your AARP membership information. This typically involves providing your AARP membership number. Ensure you enter the number accurately, including any hyphens or spaces present in your membership card.

HOW TO GET AARP DISCOUNTS ON KINDLE EBOOK

Double-check the information before proceeding to avoid any verification delays.
4. **Initiating the Verification Process:** After entering your membership number, click the button to initiate the verification process. Amazon will then communicate with AARP to confirm the validity of your membership number and your eligibility for AARP discounts.
5. **Confirmation and AARP Benefits:** Upon successful verification, a confirmation message will appear on your screen. You'll receive a notification confirming that your AARP membership is now linked to your Amazon account. This unlocks your access to discounted Kindle eBooks and potentially other AARP benefits available on the Amazon platform, depending on your membership level.

Troubleshooting Verification Issues: Solutions at Your Fingertips

In rare instances, you might encounter issues during the verification process. Here's how to troubleshoot common problems:

- **Double-check Information:** The most frequent stumbling block is inaccurate information entry. Ensure you've entered your AARP membership number precisely, including any hyphens or spaces. A single typo can cause verification failure.
- **Check Membership Status:** If entering the information correctly doesn't resolve the issue, verify that your AARP membership is active and in good standing. You can check your membership status by logging into the AARP website or contacting AARP customer support.
- **Contact Customer Support:** For any persistent verification issues, don't hesitate to reach out to either AARP or Amazon customer support. Both organizations offer dedicated phone lines and online support platforms to address your concerns.

Additional Tips for a Smooth Verification Process:

- **Maintain Updated Information:** Ensure your AARP membership

information, including your email address and contact details, is up-to-date on both the AARP website and your Amazon account. This facilitates smooth communication during the verification process.
- **Consider Multi-Factor Authentication:** For enhanced security, consider enabling multi-factor authentication (MFA) on both your AARP and Amazon accounts. This adds an extra layer of protection and can potentially prevent any unauthorized attempts to link your accounts.

Beyond Verification: Ongoing Benefits

Once you've successfully verified your AARP membership, you're ready to explore a world of discounted Kindle eBooks. Remember to keep your AARP membership active to maintain access to these savings and continue enjoying the plethora of benefits offered by AARP.

Verifying your AARP membership with Amazon is a simple but critical step that unlocks the door to significant savings on Kindle eBooks. By following these detailed instructions and troubleshooting tips, you can ensure a smooth verification process and embark on a joyous literary journey with discounted eBooks at your fingertips. So, verify your membership, explore the vast Kindle library, and embrace a world of affordable reading adventures!

Chapter 3

Identifying AARP Discounted eBooks.

Navigating the Kindle Landscape: Unveiling AARP Discounts

With your AARP membership verified and your eagerness to unlock discounted eBooks simmering, it's time to delve into the exciting world of the Kindle store. This section equips you with the knowledge to locate AARP deals and recognize discount badges, ensuring you find the best savings on your favorite reads.

The Elusive Badge: Demystifying AARP Discount Indicators

Unlike some loyalty programs, AARP discounts on Kindle eBooks aren't always explicitly displayed through prominent badges on product listings. This might seem like a hurdle, but fret not! Here's a breakdown of how AARP discounts are presented on Kindle:

1. **Scrutinizing Product Descriptions: Your Reliable Source**

   - **Keyword Recognition:** The most reliable method often involves a close examination of the eBook's product description. Look for keywords or phrases specifically mentioning "AARP Discount" or "Special Offer for AARP Members." These keywords act as clear indicators that the listed price benefits from your membership.
   - **Price Comparison:** Product descriptions sometimes mention the original price alongside the discounted price for AARP members. This direct comparison allows you to instantly recognize the savings associated with your membership. Imagine browsing a new thriller and discovering it boasts a "Special Offer for AARP Members" right next to the discounted price – a delightful surprise for your wallet!

1. **Exploring Customer Reviews (A Word of Caution):**

   - **Limited Reliability:** While not always a foolproof method, customer reviews can occasionally offer valuable insights. Some reviewers might mention utilizing AARP discounts for the specific eBook, further confirming the discounted price. However, it's crucial to approach customer reviews with a degree of caution. Not all reviewers mention their use of discounts, and the information might not always be accurate.

Beyond the Badge: Alternative Strategies for Finding Discounted Titles

While AARP discount badges might not be prominently displayed, several alternative strategies can help you identify discounted eBooks effectively:

1. **AARP as Your Guide: Utilizing AARP Resources**

   - **AARP Bookstore:** The AARP website boasts a dedicated "Bookstore" section. This valuable resource features curated lists of eBooks categorized by genre, bestseller lists, and staff recommendations – all specifically highlighting titles eligible for AARP discounts. Imagine browsing through staff picks for captivating historical fiction or exploring a curated selection of self-improvement titles, with the additional assurance that these choices come with significant savings.
   - **Newsletters and Social Media:** Subscribe to AARP's email newsletters or follow their social media pages. These platforms often announce new eBook deals and promotions, including exclusive AARP discounts. Think about discovering a highly anticipated memoir by your favorite author, only to find out it's available at a discounted price through an AARP social media post!

1. **Advanced Search Filtering on Amazon:**

   - **Price Range Filter:** While not foolproof, Amazon's advanced search filters can be helpful. Navigate to the "Kindle eBooks" section and utilize the "Price" filter. Select the "Under $[Specific Price]" option and enter a price point that typically falls within the discounted range for AARP members (often lower than the regular price). This filter helps identify potentially discounted titles, which you can then cross-check for confirmation through the methods mentioned earlier.

A Note on Price Fluctuations and Dynamic Pricing

It's important to acknowledge that eBook prices can fluctuate on Amazon. This dynamic pricing can make it challenging to definitively identify AARP discounts based solely on price comparison. However, by combining the strategies outlined in this section, you can increase your chances of finding the best deals on AARP-discounted eBooks.

While AARP discount badges might not be readily apparent, with a combination of these techniques and a little investigative spirit, you can become an adept treasure hunter in the world of discounted Kindle eBooks. Remember, a bit of research and exploration can unlock a world of affordable reading pleasure, allowing you to indulge in your literary passions without straining your budget. So, arm yourself with this knowledge, explore the treasure trove of Kindle eBooks, and embark on a rewarding adventure filled with discounted reading delights!

Recognizing AARP Discount Badges on Kindle eBooks

With your AARP membership verified and your excitement for discounted eBooks bubbling over, it's time to delve into the world of Kindle. Unlike some loyalty programs with prominent discount badges, identifying AARP-discounted eBooks might require a touch of detective work. However, fear not! This section equips you with the knowledge to recognize subtle cues and navigate the Kindle store effectively, ensuring you find the best deals on your favorite reads.

The Elusive Badge: Demystifying AA"P Discount Indicators

While AARP discounts offer significant savings, they aren't always explicitly displayed through prominent badges on individual Kindle eBook listings. This might seem like a challenge at first, but with a keen eye and the right approach, you can uncover these hidden gems. Here's a breakdown of the key methods to identify AARP-discounted eBooks:

Scrutinizing Product Descriptions: Your Reliable Source

Keyword Recognition: The most reliable method often involves a close examination of the eBook's product description. Look for specific keywords or phrases like "AARP Discount" or "Special Offer for AARP Members." These keywords act as clear indicators that the listed price benefits from your membership. Imagine browsing a captivating mystery novel and discovering the description proudly states "AARP Discount" right next to the price – a delightful surprise for your budget!

Price Comparison: Product descriptions sometimes mention the original price alongside the discounted price for AARP members. This direct comparison allows you to instantly recognize the savings associated with your membership. For instance, you might encounter a thought-provoking biography with the original price crossed out and the enticing "AARP Member Price" displayed prominently.

Exploring Customer Reviews (A Word of Caution):

Limited Reliability: While not always foolproof, customer reviews can occasionally offer valuable insights. Some reviewers might mention utilizing AARP discounts for the specific eBook, further confirming the discounted price. However, it's crucial to approach customer reviews with a degree of caution. Not all reviewers mention their use of discounts, and the information might not always be accurate. Treat customer reviews as supplementary information, not a definitive confirmation of an AARP discount.

Leveraging Third-Party Resources (Use with Caution):

Blogs and Discount Websites: Several websites and blogs track and curate lists of discounted eBooks, sometimes including AARP-specific offers. These resources can be helpful starting points for discovering discounted titles. However, proceed with caution. Not all information might be up-to-date, and some websites might be affiliated with retailers other than Amazon. Consider these resources as supplementary tools, but always double-check the information on the official AARP website or directly on Amazon before making a purchase.

Beyond the Badge: Alternative Strategies for Finding Discounted Titles

While AARP discount badges might not be prominently displayed, several alternative strategies can help you identify discounted eBooks effectively:

AARP as Your Guide: Utilizing AARP Resources

AARP Bookstore: The AARP website boasts a dedicated "Bookstore" section. This valuable resource features curated lists of eBooks categorized by genre, bestseller lists, and staff recommendations – all specifically highlighting titles eligible for AARP discounts. Imagine browsing through staff picks for captivating historical fiction or exploring a curated selection of self-improvement titles, with the additional assurance that these choices come with significant savings.

Newsletters and Social Media: Subscribe to AARP's email newsletters or follow their social media pages. These platforms often announce new eBook deals and promotions, including exclusive AARP discounts. Think about discovering a highly anticipated memoir by your favorite author, only to find out it's available at a discounted price through an AARP social media post! Social media and newsletters can act as real-time treasure maps, leading you to hidden discounts and special offers.

Advanced Search Filtering on Amazon:

Price Range Filter: While not foolproof, Amazon's advanced search filters can be helpful. Navigate to the "Kindle eBooks" section and utilize the "Price" filter. Select the "Under $[Specific Price]" option and enter a price point that typically falls within the discounted range for AARP members (often lower than the regular price). This filter helps identify potentially discounted titles, which you can then cross-check for confirmation through the methods mentioned earlier. Think of the price filter as a sifting tool, narrowing down the vast selection of eBooks to potentially discounted titles that warrant further exploration.

A Note on Price Fluctuations and D"nami' Pricing

It's important to acknowledge that eBook prices on Amazon can fluctuate due to dynamic pricing strategies. This can make it challenging to definitively identify AARP discounts based solely on price comparison. However, by combining the strategies outlined in this section, you can increase your chances of finding the best deals on AARP-discounted eBooks.

The reward of the hunt for AARP-discounted eBooks lies not just in the savings, but also in the thrill of discovery. By combining the strategies outlined in this section, you can transform yourself into a skilled "discount detective" within the Kindle store. Here's a final tip to truly elevate your AARP eBook experience:

Embrace the Journey: Think of your search for AARP-discounted eBooks as an exciting adventure. Explore different genres, delve into new authors, and rediscover old favorites. The process of unearthing hidden gems at discounted prices can be just as rewarding as the reading experience itself.

Remember, with a bit of research, exploration, and the knowledge gleaned from this section, you can navigate the world of Kindle eBooks with confidence, unlocking a treasure trove of discounted reads and enriching your literary journey with the benefits of your AARP membership. So, grab your Kindle device, unleash your inner discount detective, and embark on a rewarding adventure filled with captivating reads at affordable prices!

Utilizing AARP's Online Resources for Discounted Titles

Your AARP membership unlocks a world of benefits beyond discounted healthcare and travel. One of the hidden gems for bookworms aged 50 and above lies within AARP's online resources: a treasure trove of tools and information designed to help you discover and enjoy discounted Kindle eBooks. This section delves into the various resources offered by AARP, empowering you to navigate the online landscape and find the best deals on your next literary adventure.

The AARP Bookstore: Your Curated Gateway to Savings

Imagine a virtual bookstore specifically designed for AARP members, featuring curated selections of discounted eBooks across a vast array of genres. This dream becomes reality with the AARP Bookstore, a dedicated section within the AARP website. Here's how to leverage this valuable resource:

Browsing by Genre and Recommendation: The AARP Bookstore categorizes eBooks by genre, allowing you to explore your favorite categories like historical fiction, gripping thrillers, or insightful self-improvement guides. Each category prominently displays titles eligible for AARP discounts, ensuring you can focus on discounted selections within your preferred genre. Additionally, the AARP Bookstore features staff recommendations, highlighting captivating reads chosen by AARP experts. Imagine browsing a curated selection of "Must-Read Historical Biographies for AARP Members," knowing each title comes with the added benefit of a discounted price.

Bestseller Lists with a Discount Twist: The AARP Bookstore boasts bestseller lists specifically tailored to AARP members. These lists showcase the most popular eBooks across various genres, but with the crucial distinction of highlighting titles eligible for AARP discounts. Think about discovering the latest captivating mystery novel topping the "AARP Discounted Mystery Bestsellers" list, knowing you can enjoy this popular read at a reduced price.

Search Functionality with Discount Filters: The AARP Bookstore also offers a user-friendly search function. Utilize keywords related to your preferred genre, author, or topic. You can further refine your search by including a filter specifically for "AARP Discount" titles. This targeted search streamlines your exploration, allowing you to quickly find discounted eBooks that align with your reading interests.

Beyond the Bookstore: AARP Newsletters and Social Media

The AARP Bookstore serves as a fantastic starting point, but your exploration doesn't end there. AARP leverages the power of online communication to keep you informed about new releases, special offers, and exclusive AARP discounts on eBooks:

Newsletters: Subscribe to AARP's email newsletters, particularly those related to books or discounts. These newsletters often feature curated lists of discounted eBooks, including exclusive AARP deals. Imagine receiving an email notification highlighting a "Weekend Flash Sale" on AARP-discounted biographies, allowing you to snag a captivating read at an exceptional price.

Social Media: Follow AARP's official pages on platforms like Facebook, Twitter, or Instagram. These social media platforms are goldmines for discovering AARP discounts. AARP frequently announces new eBook deals and promotions, including exclusive AARP discounts on popular titles. Think about scrolling through your social media feed and encountering a post announcing a special discount on the new release by your favorite author, available only to AARP members!

Leveraging AARP's Content for Informed Decisions:

AARP's online resources extend beyond simply highlighting discounted titles. The website offers valuable content to empower you to make informed decisions and enhance your overall reading experience:

Book Reviews: The AARP website features book reviews written by professional reviewers and sometimes even fellow AARP members. These reviews offer valuable insights into the content, style, and overall quality of the book. Utilize these reviews to decide if a discounted eBook aligns with your reading preferences before making a purchase.

Reading Tips and Resources: AARP's online resources also delve into the realm of reading tips and tools. Explore articles on maximizing your Kindle experience, discovering new reading strategies, or even creating your own online book club with fellow AARP members. These resources enhance your overall reading journey, complementing your exploration of AARP-discounted eBooks.

Combining Resources: A Recipe for Success

The true power of AARP's online resources lies in their synergy. Here's how to combine them for optimal results:

Start with the AARP Bookstore: Browse the curated selections, explore bestseller lists specifically for discounted titles, and utilize the search function with the "AARP Discount" filter.

Stay Informed with Newsletters and Social Media: Subscribe to AARP's newsletters and follow them on social media to stay updated on new releases, special offers, and exclusive AARP discounts.

Leverage Book Reviews and Reading Tips: Utilize book reviews to make informed decisions about discounted titles and explore reading tips to enhance your overall reading experience.

By combining these resources, you create a personalized system for discovering and enjoying discounted Kindle eBooks. This empowers you to embark on a rewarding literary adventure, enriching your life with captivating reads at affordable prices.

AARP's online resources unlock a treasure trove of AARP-discounted eBooks, transforming your Kindle device into a portal to a world of affordable reading pleasure. With the AARP Bookstore as your starting point, newsletters and social media keeping you informed, and book reviews guiding your choices, you can navigate the vast world of eBooks with confidence. Remember, the journey of discovery is just as rewarding as the reading experience itself. So, embrace the thrill of the hunt, explore different genres, delve into new authors, and rediscover old favorites. With the knowledge gleaned from this section and your AARP membership, you're well on your way to becoming a master navigator in the exciting world of discounted Kindle eBooks!

Chapter 4

Identifying AARP Discounted eBooks

Percentage-Based Discounts

Having unlocked the secrets of identifying AARP-discounted eBooks, you might encounter a new layer of complexity: percentage-based discounts. Unlike some programs offering flat dollar-amount reductions, AARP discounts on Kindle eBooks often translate into percentages off the original price. This section equips you with the knowledge to decipher these percentages and maximize your savings.

The Power of Percentages: Calculating Your Savings

While a flat discount of "$5 off" is readily understandable, percentage-based discounts might require a touch of calculation. However, fret not! Understanding these percentages and calculating your savings is a straightforward process. Here's a breakdown of the key points:

Locating the Discount Percentage: The first step involves identifying the actual discount percentage associated with the AARP offer. This information can be found in several locations:

Product Description: The product description for the AARP-discounted eBook on Amazon might explicitly mention the discount percentage. Look for phrases like "20% off for AARP Members" or "Enjoy a 35% AARP Discount."

AARP Bookstore: If you discovered the discounted title through the AARP Bookstore, the website might display the discount percentage alongside the title information.

AARP Newsletters or Social Media: Newsletters or social media announcements from AARP might highlight a specific percentage discount for a particular eBook or even a broader promotion offering a set discount on a category of eBooks.

Performing the Math (Simplified Approach):

Once you've located the discount percentage, calculating your savings becomes simple. Here's a simplified approach:

- Identify the Original Price: Locate the original price of the eBook on Amazon (listed before the discount is applied).

- Multiply the Discount Percentage: Multiply the original price by the discount percentage (expressed as a decimal). For example, if the original price is $10.00 and the discount is 20%, you'd multiply $10.00 by 0.2 (which is 20% converted to a decimal).

- Subtract the Result: Subtract the result you obtained in step two from the original price. This will give you the amount of savings you'll enjoy with your AARP discount.

Illustrative Examples: Calculating Savings in Action

Here are some illustrative examples to solidify your understanding:

Example 1: A 20% Discount on a $15.00 eBook: Following the steps outlined above:

Original Price: $15.00

Discount Percentage: 20% (expressed as a decimal: 0.2)

Savings Calculation: $15.00 x 0.2 = $3.00

Discounted Price for AARP Member: $15.00 (original price) - $3.00 (savings) = $12.00

Example 2: A 35% Discount on a $7.99 eBook: Following the same steps:

Original Price: $7.99

Discount Percentage: 35% (expressed as a decimal: 0.35)

Savings Calculation: $7.99 x 0.35 = $2.79 (rounded to nearest cent)

Discounted Price for AARP Member: $7.99 (original price) - $2.79 (savings) = $5.20

Additional Tips for Utilizing Percentage-Based Discounts:

Here are some extra strategies to maximize your savings with percentage-based AARP discounts:

Compare Prices Across Retailers: While AARP discounts are significant, it's always a good practice to compare prices with other retailers before making a purchase. However, keep in mind that AARP discounts might be exclusive to Amazon.

Consider Bundle Deals: Sometimes, retailers offer bundle deals for multiple eBooks. If you're interested in purchasing several AARP-discounted titles, explore bundle options, as they might offer additional savings compared to buying each book individually.

Prioritize Higher-Priced eBooks: When faced with multiple AARP-discounted titles, consider prioritizing those with a higher original price. The percentage discount translates to a greater dollar-amount saving for more expensive eBooks.

By understanding how to interpret and calculate percentage-based discounts, you've unlocked another key to maximizing your AARP benefits on Kindle eBooks. Remember, a little math can go a long way in stretching your book budget further, allowing you to indulge in more captivating reads at a reduced cost.

Fixed-Amount Discounts

In the world of AARP discounts on Kindle eBooks, you might encounter another enticing offer: fixed-amount discounts. Unlike percentage-based reductions, these discounts translate to a specific dollar amount shaved off the original price. This section delves into the details of fixed-amount AARP discounts, empowering you to identify these deals and make the most of your savings.

Spotting the Savings: Identifying Fixed-Amount AARP Discounts

While percentage-based discounts might require some calculation, fixed-amount AARP discounts are readily apparent. Here's how to identify these deals on Kindle eBooks:

Product Description: The product description for the AARP-discounted eBook often takes center stage when it comes to highlighting fixed-amount savings. Look for phrases like "$3.00 off for AARP Members" or "Enjoy a Special Offer: Save $5.00 with AARP." Imagine browsing the Kindle store and encountering a captivating novel with the description boasting "AARP Members Save $2.00!" – a clear indicator of the discount you'll receive.

AARP Bookstore: The AARP Bookstore can be a treasure trove for fixed-amount AARP discounts. Curated lists and bestseller sections might showcase titles with the specific dollar amount you'll save as an AARP member. Think about browsing the "AARP Discounted Travel Memoirs" section and discovering each title proudly displays "Save $4.99 with AARP!"

AARP Announcements: Newsletters and social media posts from AARP might highlight special promotions featuring fixed-amount discounts on specific eBooks or even a broader category. Imagine receiving an email notification announcing "AARP Weekend Sale: Save $2.00 on All Self-Help eBooks!"

The Art of Comparison: Maximizing Savings with Fixed-Amount Discounts

While fixed-amount discounts are easy to understand, a little strategizing can help you maximize your savings. Here are some valuable tips:

Consider the Original Price: The true value of a fixed-amount discount hinges on the original price of the eBook. A $3.00 discount might seem significant for a $5.99 eBook but less impactful for a $19.99 title.

Prioritize Higher-Priced eBooks: When faced with multiple AARP-discounted titles with fixed-amount savings, prioritize those with a higher original price. The fixed discount translates to a greater percentage saving on more expensive eBooks.

Compare Across Retailers (with Caution): It's always a good practice to compare prices with other retailers before making a purchase. However, keep in mind that AARP discounts might be exclusive to Amazon. Additionally, factor in any potential shipping costs from other retailers when comparing prices.

Illustrative Examples: Understanding the Impact of Fixed-Amount Discounts

Here are some examples to illustrate the impact of fixed-amount discounts on different priced eBooks:

Example 1: A $3.00 Discount on a $5.99 eBook: This discount translates to a significant saving of nearly 50% (since $3.00 represents almost half of the original $5.99 price).

Example 2: A $3.00 Discount on a $14.99 eBook: The discount represents a saving of approximately 20% (because $3.00 divided by $14.99 is roughly 0.20).

Example 3: A $5.00 Discount on a $19.99 eBook: This discount translates to a saving of around 25% (since $5.00 divided by $19.99 is approximately 0.25).

As you can see, fixed-amount discounts can be particularly attractive for higher-priced eBooks, offering a significant percentage saving that translates to substantial cost reduction.

Combining Strategies for Optimal Savings

The true power of AARP discounts lies in combining different strategies. Here's how to create a winning formula:

Look for Fixed-Amount Discounts: Prioritize titles boasting fixed-amount AARP savings, especially for higher-priced eBooks.

Consider Percentage-Based Discounts (Optional): If you encounter an AARP discount with a percentage instead of a fixed amount, utilize the calculation methods from the previous section to assess the potential savings.

Compare Prices (with Caution): Do a quick price comparison with other retailers, keeping in mind AARP discounts might be exclusive to Amazon and considering any potential shipping costs.

By combining these strategies, you can make informed decisions, identify the best deals, and maximize your savings on AARP-discounted Kindle eBooks.

Limited-Time Offers and Daily Deals

The world of AARP discounts on Kindle eBooks extends beyond static price reductions. AARP and Amazon often collaborate to offer exciting limited-time promotions and daily deals, adding a layer of thrill to your search for discounted reads. This section equips you with the knowledge to identify these fleeting opportunities and maximize your savings on captivating eBooks.

The Elusive Deals: Unveiling Limited-Time AARP Offers

Imagine browsing the Kindle store and encountering a banner announcing a "Special AARP Weekend Sale!" or receiving an email notification highlighting a "Flash Sale on AARP-Discounted Biographies!" These are just a few examples of limited-time AARP offers that can unlock incredible savings on a variety of eBooks. Here's how to stay informed and capitalize on these fleeting opportunities:

- **AARP Newsletters and Social Media:** Be sure to subscribe to AARP's email newsletters and follow their social media pages (Facebook, Twitter, Instagram). These platforms serve as your primary source of information regarding limited-time AARP offers. AARP frequently announces these promotions through these channels, highlighting the specific discounted titles, the duration of the offer, and the percentage or fixed-amount savings you can enjoy.
- **AARP Website Announcements:** Keep an eye out for announcements and special banners displayed prominently on the AARP website. Similar to social media and newsletters, these announcements can showcase limited-time AARP offers, guiding you towards discounted eBooks within a specific timeframe.

- **Kindle Store Exploration:** While browsing the Kindle store, especially during peak shopping seasons (like holidays), be on the lookout for special promotions or banners highlighting limited-time AARP offers. These might be displayed on the Kindle store's homepage or within specific categories (e.g., "Biographies" or "Mystery").

The Daily Deal Dilemma: Navigating AARP-Discounted Daily Deals

While less common, AARP occasionally collaborates with Amazon to offer daily deals on specific eBooks. These deals offer significant discounts for a limited time, typically lasting 24 hours. Here's what you need to know about navigating daily deals:

- **Limited Availability:** The key characteristic of daily deals is their fleeting nature. The discounted eBook might only be available at the reduced price for a single day, so acting quickly is essential.
- **Identifying Daily Deals:** There's no single, definitive location to find AARP-discounted daily deals. However, the strategies mentioned above for uncovering limited-time offers can also be applied to daily deals. Keep an eye on AARP newsletters, social media, the AARP website, and even the Kindle store itself for any announcements or banners highlighting a daily deal.
- **Quick Decision-Making:** Since daily deals are time-sensitive, be prepared to make a quick decision on whether to purchase the discounted eBook. Utilize the knowledge you've gained from this book to assess the savings (percentage-based or fixed-amount) and compare the overall price with other retailers (keeping in mind potential AARP exclusivity and shipping costs).

Maximizing Savings with Limited-Time Offers and Daily Deals

Here are some additional tips to maximize your savings with both limited-time offers and daily deals:

- **Prioritize Genres You Enjoy:** Limited-time offers often encompass a variety of genres. Focus on promotions that feature discounted titles within your preferred reading categories to ensure you're maximizing your savings on books you'll truly enjoy.
- **Combine with Other Strategies:** Don't hesitate to combine limited-time offers and daily deals with the other discount-finding strategies outlined in this book. For instance, you might encounter a limited-time offer for a fixed-amount discount on an eBook already boasting a percentage-based AARP discount!
- **Consider Bundle Deals:** If a limited-time offer or daily deal features a collection of AARP-discounted eBooks bundled together, explore the option. Bundles often offer additional savings compared to purchasing each eBook individually.

The Enchantment of the Hunt: Embracing the Thrill

Limited-time offers and daily deals add a layer of excitement to your search for AARP-discounted eBooks. By staying informed through AARP's communication channels and exploring the Kindle store regularly, you can become an adept hunter for these fleeting opportunities. Remember, the thrill of the hunt and the joy of discovering a captivating read at a significant discount are just as rewarding as the reading experience itself.

Conclusion: A Symphony of Savings Awaits

With the knowledge gleaned from this section, you're well-equipped to navigate the dynamic world of AARP discounts on Kindle eBooks. By combining strategies for identifying fixed-amount and percentage-based discounts, keeping an eye out for limited-time offers and daily deals, and prioritizing titles within your reading interests, you can create a symphony of savings.

The world of AARP discounts on Kindle eBooks extends beyond static price reductions. AARP and Amazon often collaborate to offer exciting limited-time promotions and daily deals, adding a layer of thrill to your search for

HOW TO GET AARP DISCOUNTS ON KINDLE EBOOK

discounted reads. This section equips you with the knowledge to identify these fleeting opportunities and maximize your savings on captivating eBooks.

The Elusive Deals: Unveiling Limited-Time AARP Offers

Imagine browsing the Kindle store and encountering a banner announcing a "Special AARP Weekend Sale!" or receiving an email notification highlighting a "Flash Sale on AARP-Discounted Biographies!" These are just a few examples of limited-time AARP offers that can unlock incredible savings on a variety of eBooks. Here's how to stay informed and capitalize on these fleeting opportunities:

AARP Newsletters and Social Media: Be sure to subscribe to AARP's email newsletters and follow their social media pages (Facebook, Twitter, Instagram). These platforms serve as your primary source of information regarding limited-time AARP offers. AARP frequently announces these promotions through these channels, highlighting the specific discounted titles, the duration of the offer, and the percentage or fixed-amount savings you can enjoy.

AARP Website Announcements: Keep an eye out for announcements and special banners displayed prominently on the AARP website. Similar to social media and newsletters, these announcements can showcase limited-time AARP offers, guiding you towards discounted eBooks within a specific timeframe.

Kindle Store Exploration: While browsing the Kindle store, especially during peak shopping seasons (like holidays), be on the lookout for special promotions or banners highlighting limited-time AARP offers. These might be displayed on the Kindle store's homepage or within specific categories (e.g., "Biographies" or "Mystery").

The Daily Deal Dilemma: Navigating AARP-Discounted Daily Deals

While less common, AARP occasionally collaborates with Amazon to offer daily deals on specific eBooks. These deals offer significant discounts for a limited time, typically lasting 24 hours. Here's what you need to know about navigating daily deals:

Limited Availability: The key characteristic of daily deals is their fleeting nature. The discounted eBook might only be available at the reduced price for a single day, so acting quickly is essential.

Identifying Daily Deals: There's no single, definitive location to find AARP-discounted daily deals. However, the strategies mentioned above for uncovering limited-time offers can also be applied to daily deals. Keep an eye on AARP newsletters, social media, the AARP website, and even the Kindle store itself for any announcements or banners highlighting a daily deal.

Quick Decision-Making: Since daily deals are time-sensitive, be prepared to make a quick decision on whether to purchase the discounted eBook. Utilize the knowledge you've gained from this book to assess the savings (percentage-based or fixed-amount) and compare the overall price with other retailers (keeping in mind potential AARP exclusivity and shipping costs).

Maximizing Savings with Limited-Time Offers and Daily Deals

Here are some additional tips to maximize your savings with both limited-time offers and daily deals:

Prioritize Genres You Enjoy: Limited-time offers often encompass a variety of genres. Focus on promotions that feature discounted titles within your preferred reading categories to ensure you're maximizing your savings on books you'll truly enjoy.

Combine with Other Strategies: Don't hesitate to combine limited-time offers and daily deals with the other discount-finding strategies outlined in this book. For instance, you might encounter a limited-time offer for a fixed-amount discount on an eBook already boasting a percentage-based AARP discount!

Consider Bundle Deals: If a limited-time offer or daily deal features a collection of AARP-discounted eBooks bundled together, explore the option. Bundles often offer additional savings compared to purchasing each eBook individually.

The Enchantment of the Hunt: Embracing the Thrill

Limited-time offers and daily deals add a layer of excitement to your search for AARP-discounted eBooks. By staying informed through AARP's communication channels and exploring the Kindle store regularly, you can become an adept hunter for these fleeting opportunities. Remember, the thrill of the hunt and the joy of discovering a captivating read at a significant discount are just as rewarding as the reading experience itself.

With the knowledge gleaned from this section, you're well-equipped to navigate the dynamic world of AARP discounts on Kindle eBooks. By combining strategies for identifying fixed-amount and percentage-based discounts, keeping an eye out for limited-time offers and daily deals, and prioritizing titles within your reading interests, you can create a symphony of savings.

Chapter 5

Advanced Search Techniques for Finding AARP Discounted eBooks

Using AARP Membership Number During Search

Throughout this guide, we've explored various strategies for uncovering AARP-discounted eBooks within the vast expanse of the Kindle store. One common misconception involves the notion of directly utilizing your AARP membership number during the search process. This section clarifies this misconception and offers alternative approaches to ensure you leverage your AARP membership for optimal savings.

Why You Can't Search with Your AARP Number:

The Amazon Kindle store search functionality isn't currently designed to integrate directly with your AARP membership number. While some online platforms might require membership numbers for login or accessing exclusive features, searching for AARP-discounted eBooks on the Kindle store requires a different approach.

Alternative Strategies for Discount Discovery:

Here are effective tactics to identify AARP-discounted titles without needing your membership number during the search:

Focus on AARP Resources: Your AARP membership unlocks a treasure trove of resources specifically designed to highlight AARP-discounted eBooks. Leverage these resources as your primary starting point:

The AARP Bookstore: As a curated online platform within the AARP website, the AARP Bookstore showcases a vast selection of eBooks with AARP discounts. Browse by genre, bestseller lists, or explore staff recommendations, all featuring titles eligible for discounted purchase with your AARP membership.

AARP Newsletters and Social Media: Stay informed about new releases, special offers, and exclusive AARP discounts on eBooks by subscribing to AARP's email newsletters and following their social media pages. These channels serve as valuable sources of information, highlighting discounted titles and providing direct links to purchase them on the Kindle store.

Utilize Advanced Search Techniques: Mastering advanced search techniques on the Kindle store empowers you to identify eBooks with the potential for AARP discounts. Techniques covered in the previous section of this guide, such as price filters, category filters, and keyword filters, can be combined to create a personalized search strategy for uncovering discounted titles.

Scrutinize Product Descriptions: Once you've identified potential AARP-discounted titles, delve deeper by examining the product descriptions. Look for keywords like "AARP Discount" or price comparisons highlighting the discounted price for AARP members. This verification ensures you're taking advantage of the savings before making a purchase.

Beyond Search: Additional Resources for Discounted Reads

While searching is an effective approach, remember other avenues to explore:

Customer Reviews (with Caution): While not definitive proof, some customer reviews might mention utilizing AARP discounts for a specific eBook. However, approach this information with caution, as review accuracy can vary.

Online Book Review Websites: Some online book review websites might include information about potential AARP discounts for specific titles. However, prioritize information directly from AARP resources or the product descriptions on the Kindle store.

While you can't directly search with your AARP membership number, the strategies outlined in this section empower you to leverage your AARP membership effectively. Remember, the journey of discovery and the thrill of finding a captivating discounted read are just as rewarding as the reading experience itself. So, delve into the treasure trove of AARP resources, explore advanced search techniques, and embark on a literary adventure filled with affordable and enriching reads!

Filtering by Category and Genre

The vast library of the Kindle store can feel overwhelming when searching for AARP-discounted eBooks. Here's where strategic filtering by category and genre becomes your secret weapon. This section equips you with the knowledge to navigate the Kindle store's filters and pinpoint AARP-discounted titles that align perfectly with your reading preferences.

The Power of Categories: Organizing the Kindle Store by Subject

Imagine a library with designated sections for fiction, history, and biographies. Categories on the Kindle store function similarly, organizing eBooks into broad subject areas. Here's how to leverage them effectively in your search for AARP discounts:

Browsing by Category: On the Kindle store's homepage, you'll find a prominent "Browse" category list. Clicking on this list reveals a multitude of categories encompassing various genres and subjects (e.g., Mystery, Romance, Self-Help, History).

Refine Your Search: Once you select a particular category, you've narrowed down your search considerably. This initial filtering ensures you're exploring AARP-discounted titles within your preferred subject area.

Exploring Subcategories (Optional): Some categories on the Kindle store offer further refinement through subcategories. For example, the "Mystery" category might have subcategories for "Cozy Mysteries," "Police Procedurals," or "Thrillers." Utilize subcategories to delve even deeper into your area of interest.

Genre Finesse: Unveiling AARP Gems Within Categories

While categories provide a broad subject area, genres allow for even more specific filtering. Here's how genres can guide you towards AARP-discounted titles you'll truly enjoy:

Genre Filters: Many category pages on the Kindle store will present a sidebar with a list of relevant genres. Clicking on a specific genre refines your search further, ensuring you're exploring AARP-discounted titles within your preferred genre (e.g., Historical Romance, Science Fiction Thriller, Memoir).

Combining Category and Genre: The true power lies in combining category and genre filters. For instance, you might start by browsing the "Romance" category and then utilize the genre filter to select "Historical Romance" if that's your preferred subgenre. This approach significantly narrows down your search results, focusing on AARP-discounted titles that perfectly match your reading interests.

Beyond the Basics: Advanced Filtering Techniques

The Kindle store offers some additional filtering features that can further enhance your search for AARP discounts:

Availability: Use the "Availability" filter to focus on eBooks available for purchase (excluding Kindle Unlimited titles or rentals). This ensures you're only browsing titles you can potentially purchase with your AARP discount.

Sort by Price: While AARP discounts can vary, they often translate to a reduced price. Utilize the "Sort by Price" filter (low to high) to prioritize titles within a price range that might indicate AARP discounts. However, remember that this is not a foolproof method, and further verification might be required (as explained in later sections of this guide).

Leveraging Customer Reviews (with Caution):

While not a definitive confirmation of an AARP discount, some customer reviews might mention using an AARP discount for a specific eBook. However, approach this information with caution as the accuracy of reviews can vary. It's always best to prioritize verification methods outlined in later sections of this guide.

Combining Techniques for Maximum Efficiency

Here's a winning formula to maximize your search efficiency:

Start with a Broad Category: Begin by selecting a general category that aligns with your reading preferences (e.g., Fiction, Non-Fiction).

Refine with Genre Filters: Once within the category, utilize genre filters to narrow down your search to your preferred subgenre (e.g., Historical Fiction, Self-Help for Beginners).

Apply Additional Filters (Optional): Consider using the "Availability" filter to focus on purchasable eBooks and the "Sort by Price" filter (low to high) to potentially target AARP-discounted titles.

Examine Product Descriptions: After filtering, don't forget to scrutinize the product descriptions for each shortlisted eBook. Look for keywords like "AARP Discount" or price comparisons highlighting the discounted price for AARP members.

Beyond Filtering: Exploring Additional Avenues

While filtering by category and genre is a powerful tool, remember there are other avenues to explore for AARP-discounted eBooks:

The AARP Bookstore: This curated platform within the AARP website showcases a vast selection of eBooks with AARP discounts. Browse by category or genre to discover discounted titles that align perfectly with your interests.

Combining Search Terms with "AARP Discount

The vast library of the Kindle store holds countless AARP-discounted gems waiting to be discovered. This section delves into the art of combining search terms with "AARP Discount" to refine your search and unearth discounted eBooks that pique your literary curiosity.

Beyond the Obvious: Delving Deeper than "AARP Discount"

While including "AARP Discount" in your search terms can be effective, it's not the only strategy. Here's why, and how to expand your search horizons:

- **Limited Scope:** Relying solely on "AARP Discount" might limit

your search results. Not all AARP-discounted titles explicitly mention the discount in their product descriptions.
- **False Positives:** Some titles might include "AARP Discount" in their description for various reasons, not necessarily because they're part of an official AARP discount program.

Expanding Your Search Vocabulary: Alternative Keywords

Here's a treasure trove of alternative keywords to consider incorporating into your search terms:

- **"Senior Discount":** This term often aligns with AARP-discounted titles, catering to a similar demographic.
- **Author-Specific Keywords:** If you're a fan of a particular author known to participate in AARP discount programs, include their name alongside "AARP Discount" or "Senior Discount" in your search.
- **Genre-Specific Keywords:** Combine genre keywords with "AARP Discount" or "Senior Discount" in your search. For instance, searching for "Travel Memoirs AARP Discount" might lead you to discounted travel memoirs appealing to the AARP demographic.
- **"Special Offer for AARP Members":** This keyword targets titles that explicitly mention AARP membership benefits in their product descriptions.

Crafting Effective Search Queries: Combining Terms for Success

Here's how to strategically combine your chosen keywords to create effective search queries:

- **Start with Broad Genre or Category:** Begin by selecting a broad category or genre that aligns with your reading preferences (e.g., "Mystery" or "Historical Fiction").
- **Incorporate Keyword Combinations:** Within your chosen category or genre, utilize quotation marks to create targeted search queries. For

instance, try "Mystery" +"AARP Discount" or "Historical Fiction" +"Senior Discount."
- **Explore Multiple Keywords:** Experiment with different keyword combinations. You might find success searching for "Travel Memoirs" +"Special Offer for AARP Members" or even broader queries like "Biography" +"AARP Discount" OR "Senior Discount."

Beyond Basic Search: Advanced Techniques for Combining Terms

The Kindle store offers additional tools to refine your search when combining terms:

- **Utilize Boolean Operators (Optional):** For more advanced searches, consider using Boolean operators like "AND" and "OR" to combine keywords. For example, the search query "Mystery" +"AARP Discount" AND "Published 2023" refines your search to include only AARP-discounted mysteries published in 2023.
- **Leverage the "Search Within Results" Feature:** Once you have a set of initial results, utilize the "Search Within Results" feature. This allows you to search for specific keywords (like "AARP Discount" or "Senior Discount") within the existing list, further narrowing down your options to potentially discounted titles.

Verifying Your Finds: The Final Step

After employing these search strategies, you'll likely encounter a curated list of eBooks with potential AARP discounts. Here's how to verify your finds:

- **Scrutinize Product Descriptions:** Carefully examine the product description for each eBook. Look for keywords like "AARP Discount," price comparisons highlighting the discounted price for AARP members, or mentions of participation in an AARP discount program.
- **Double-Check with AARP Resources:** If you discovered the title through an AARP source (e.g., Bookstore, newsletter), you can be

more confident about the discount. However, for titles identified solely through keyword searches, consider checking the AARP website or social media for any mention of the specific discount.

Beyond Search: Complementary Strategies

While combining search terms is a powerful tool, remember other avenues to explore for AARP-discounted eBooks:

- **The AARP Bookstore:** This curated platform showcases AARP-discounted titles across various genres. Browse by category or bestseller lists to discover discounted titles that might not be easily identifiable through keyword searches.
- **AARP Newsletters and Social Media:** Stay informed about new releases, special offers, and exclusive AARP discounts through AARP's communication channels. These sources often highlight discounted titles with specific links, saving you the time and effort of searching.

Chapter 6

The Kindle Purchase Process with AARP Discounts.

Adding Discounted eBooks to Your Cart.

Having identified a treasure trove of AARP-discounted eBooks, the next step is adding them to your Kindle cart for a streamlined purchase experience. This section equips you with the knowledge to navigate the Kindle store's cart functionality and ensure your discounted reads are secured with ease.

Understanding the Cart: Your Temporary eBook Holding Area

Imagine a virtual shopping basket for your eBooks. That's essentially what the Kindle store's cart functions as. Here's what you need to know:

- **Adding eBooks to the Cart:** Once you've identified an AARP-discounted eBook (after verification through product descriptions or AARP resources), locate the "Add to Cart" button on the product page. Clicking this button adds the eBook to your virtual shopping basket.
- **Viewing Your Cart:** To access your cart and review the eBooks you've selected, locate the "Cart" icon or link (usually at the top right corner) on the Kindle store homepage or any product page. Clicking on this icon takes you to a dedicated cart page where you can manage your selections.
- **Managing Your Cart:** The cart page displays a list of all eBooks you've added, including their titles, prices (reflecting the AARP discount, if applicable), and cover images. You can also modify the quantities (if purchasing multiple copies) or remove unwanted titles from your cart using the provided options.

Maximizing Cart Efficiency: Strategic Considerations

Here are some tips to ensure your cart functions effectively and streamlines your purchase of AARP-discounted eBooks:

- **Combine Discounts for Additional Savings:** While AARP discounts are substantial, explore the possibility of combining them with other promotions or deals offered on the Kindle store. For instance, you might encounter a "Weekend Flash Sale" offering an additional percentage discount on AARP-discounted titles already in your cart.
- **Utilize "Move to Save for Later" (Optional):** If you're unsure about purchasing an AARP-discounted eBook immediately, consider using the "Move to Save for Later" option (available on the product page or cart). This creates a separate list where you can store titles for future consideration without removing them from your search results.
- **Monitor Cart Expiration (if applicable):** While uncommon, some promotional AARP discounts might have a limited time window for adding discounted titles to your cart. Pay close attention to any expiration notices displayed on the product page or within your cart to avoid missing out on a discounted purchase.

The Art of the Checkout: Securing Your Discounted eBooks

Once you've finalized your cart selections and ensured all AARP discounts are reflected, you're ready to proceed to checkout. Here's what to expect:

- **Initiating Checkout:** On the cart page, locate the "Proceed to Checkout" button. Clicking this button takes you to the checkout process.
- **Payment Information:** During checkout, you'll be prompted to enter or confirm your preferred payment method linked to your Amazon account. Ensure this information is accurate to avoid any delays in processing your purchase of AARP-discounted eBooks.
- **Final Confirmation:** Before finalizing your purchase, the checkout process provides a final overview of your cart contents, including

titles, quantities, and the total price reflecting the applied AARP discounts. Review these details carefully to ensure accuracy before confirming your order.

Beyond the Basics: Troubleshooting Potential Cart Issues

While the Kindle store's cart system is user-friendly, here are some troubleshooting tips in case you encounter any issues:

- **Missing Discounts:** If an AARP discount isn't reflected in your cart, double-check the product description and verify your AARP membership status. If the issue persists, contact Kindle customer service for assistance.
- **Cart Synchronization:** If you're accessing your cart from different devices (e.g., computer, phone), it might take a few moments for your selections to synchronize across all platforms. Be patient and allow some time for the cart to update across devices.
- **Expired Discounts:** If you encounter an error message regarding an expired discount, remove the affected title from your cart and search for it again. The AARP discount might no longer be valid on that specific title.

By mastering the art of adding discounted eBooks to your cart, you ensure a streamlined and efficient purchase experience. Remember, the Kindle store's cart system is your valuable ally in securing AARP-discounted reads. So, explore these functionalities, employ the strategies outlined in this section, and embark on a rewarding journey of literary discovery, all while maximizing your savings with AARP discounts!

Verifying AARP Discount Application at Checkout.

You've meticulously scoured the Kindle store, employed advanced search techniques, and unearthed a treasure trove of AARP-discounted eBooks. You've carefully curated your cart, ensuring titles and quantities reflect your literary desires. Now comes the crucial moment: checkout. This section equips you with the knowledge to verify the successful application of your AARP discount at checkout, guaranteeing you secure those savings on your captivating reads.

Understanding the Checkout Process: A Glimpse Behind the Scenes

Imagine a behind-the-scenes system that verifies your AARP membership and applies the corresponding discount to your chosen eBooks. That's essentially what happens during the Kindle store checkout process. Here's a breakdown of the key steps:

- **AARP Membership Verification (Optional):** While not always required, the checkout process might prompt you to verify your AARP membership status. This verification might involve logging in to your AARP account or providing a membership ID (if applicable).
- **Discount Calculation:** Behind the scenes, the checkout system checks your AARP membership status (if verification was required) and retrieves the applicable discount information for each AARP-discounted eBook in your cart.
- **Price Adjustment and Display:** The system then calculates the discounted price for each AARP-discounted eBook by subtracting the appropriate discount percentage or fixed amount from the original price. This discounted price is then reflected in your checkout summary.

Keeping a Watchful Eye: Verifying the Applied Discount

It's crucial to verify that the AARP discounts have been accurately applied to your eBooks at checkout. Here's what to look for:

- **Review Your Cart Summary:** Before finalizing your purchase, the checkout process displays a detailed summary of your cart contents. This summary includes the title, quantity, and most importantly, the price of each eBook. Pay close attention to the price displayed for AARP-discounted titles.

- **Compare with Original Price:** Recall the original price you saw on the product page before adding the eBook to your cart. Compare this original price with the discounted price displayed in your checkout summary. The difference should reflect the AARP discount percentage or fixed amount.
- **Discount Breakdown (Optional):** In some cases, the checkout process might offer a breakdown of applied discounts. Look for a section mentioning "AARP Discount" and the corresponding amount deducted from the original price.

Troubleshooting Discrepancies: Resolving AARP Discount Issues

If you suspect an error in the application of your AARP discount at checkout, here are some troubleshooting steps:

- **Double-Check Membership Status:** Ensure your AARP membership is active and in good standing. You can verify this by logging into your AARP account.
- **Review Product Description:** Revisit the product page for the AARP-discounted eBook in question. Scrutinize the product description to ensure the discount is still valid and hasn't expired.
- **Contact Kindle Customer Service:** If, after verifying your membership and product information, you're still encountering issues with the AARP discount application, don't hesitate to contact Kindle customer service. Explain the situation clearly and provide any relevant details (e.g., product titles, screenshots) to assist them in resolving the problem.

Beyond Verification: Additional Tips for Checkout Success

Here are some additional tips to ensure a smooth and successful checkout experience:

- **Ensure Stable Internet Connection:** A stable internet connection is crucial for a seamless checkout process. A weak connection might

cause delays or errors, hindering the verification of your AARP membership or the application of discounts.
- **Review Payment Information:** Before finalizing your purchase, double-check your payment information to ensure accuracy. This includes verifying the linked payment method and ensuring sufficient funds are available for the discounted total amount.
- **Utilize Two-Factor Authentication (Optional):** If enabled on your account, consider using two-factor authentication for added security during checkout. This might involve entering a code received through text message or email to verify your purchase.

By understanding the checkout process and actively verifying the application of your AARP discount, you can approach your purchase with confidence. Remember, a little vigilance at checkout ensures you secure the well-deserved savings on your AARP-discounted eBooks. So, with this knowledge under your belt, embark on your literary adventure, reveling in the joy of reading while maximizing your savings with AARP discounts!

Payment Options for Kindle Purchases.

Having meticulously identified AARP-discounted eBooks, navigated the intricacies of the cart system, and verified discount application at checkout, you're almost ready to embark on your literary journey. This section delves into the various payment options available for purchasing AARP-discounted eBooks on the Kindle store, ensuring a smooth and secure transaction.

Understanding Payment Methods: A World of Convenience

The Kindle store offers a wide range of payment options to cater to your individual preferences. Here's a breakdown of some popular methods:

- **Credit Cards:** Widely accepted for online purchases, credit cards offer a convenient way to pay for your AARP-discounted eBooks. You can link your preferred credit card to your Amazon account for a

streamlined checkout process.
- **Debit Cards:** Similar to credit cards, debit cards allow for direct payment from your linked bank account. Ensure sufficient funds are available in your account to cover the discounted total for your AARP eBooks.
- **Amazon Gift Cards:** If you have an Amazon gift card with sufficient balance to cover the purchase, you can redeem it at checkout for your AARP-discounted eBooks. This can be a great way to utilize existing gift cards and maximize your savings.
- **1-Click Payment (Optional):** For a truly streamlined experience, consider enabling 1-Click payment on your Amazon account. This allows you to store your preferred payment information for future purchases, eliminating the need to re-enter details during checkout for subsequent AARP-discounted eBooks.

Choosing the Right Payment Method: Factors to Consider

While all the mentioned methods allow for purchasing AARP-discounted eBooks, here are some factors to consider when selecting your preferred option:

- **Security:** Prioritize payment methods that offer robust security features. Credit cards with chip and pin technology or debit cards with two-factor authentication provide additional layers of protection for your financial information.
- **Convenience:** Consider how convenient a method is for you. 1-Click payment offers ultimate ease, while credit or debit cards might require you to enter details during checkout.
- **Budgeting:** If you're on a budget, using a debit card ensures you only spend the funds available in your account. Credit cards offer more flexibility but require responsible management to avoid overspending.
- **Gift Card Balance:** If you have an Amazon gift card with sufficient balance, using it can be a convenient way to manage your spending and avoid using other payment methods.

Beyond the Basics: Exploring Additional Payment Options

While the methods mentioned above are popular choices, here are some additional options to consider:

- **Amazon Points:** If you're an active Amazon user and participate in the Amazon Points program, you might have accumulated points redeemable towards purchases. Consider using these points to offset the cost of your AARP-discounted eBooks.
- **Promotional Credits:** Occasionally, Amazon offers promotional credits applicable towards eBook purchases. If you have such credits available, you can redeem them at checkout to further reduce the cost of AARP-discounted titles.

Security First: Safeguarding Your Payment Information

Here are some crucial tips to ensure the security of your payment information when purchasing AARP-discounted eBooks:

- **Shop on Secure Websites:** Always ensure you're on the official Kindle store website (amazon.com) during checkout. Look for the padlock symbol in your browser's address bar, indicating a secure connection.
- **Beware of Phishing Attempts:** Phishing emails or websites might try to mimic the Kindle store and trick you into revealing your payment information. Be cautious of unsolicited emails and only access the Kindle store through the official website.
- **Review Transaction History:** Regularly review your transaction history on your Amazon account to ensure all purchases, including AARP-discounted eBooks, are legitimate.

By understanding the different payment options and prioritizing security measures, you can approach your purchase of AARP-discounted eBooks with confidence. Remember, the chosen payment method should cater to your individual needs and comfort level. So, with this knowledge at hand, finalize your purchase, secure your discounted reads, and delve into the captivating world of AARP-discounted eBooks!

Chapter 7

Troubleshooting Common Issues with AARP Discounts.

Resolving Membership Verification Errors.

The thrill of discovering AARP-discounted eBooks can be dampened by encountering a membership verification error at checkout. But fear not! This section equips you with the knowledge and troubleshooting steps to resolve these errors and secure your well-deserved savings.

Understanding Membership Verification: The Gatekeeper of Discounts

The Kindle store checkout process might require verification of your AARP membership status before applying AARP discounts to your eBooks. This verification ensures the discounts are applied to eligible users. Here are some reasons why you might encounter an error:

Inactive or Expired Membership: The most common reason is an inactive or expired AARP membership. Ensure your membership is current and in good standing to qualify for AARP discounts on Kindle eBooks.

Incorrect Account Information: Double-check that the information used during checkout (e.g., email address) matches the details associated with your AARP membership. A mismatch can lead to verification errors.

Technical Glitches (Uncommon): While less frequent, technical glitches on the Kindle store's side might occasionally cause verification errors. These are typically resolved quickly by Amazon.

Troubleshooting Techniques: Unlocking the AARP Discount Gate

Here's a step-by-step approach to resolving membership verification errors and securing your AARP discounts:

Verify AARP Membership Status: Begin by logging into your AARP account and verifying your membership status. Ensure your membership is active and hasn't expired.

Check Checkout Information: Carefully review the information you entered during checkout on the Kindle store. Confirm that the email address or any other required details match those associated with your AARP membership.

Clear Browser Cache and Cookies (Optional): In rare instances, outdated browser cache or cookies might interfere with the verification process. Try clearing your browser cache and cookies, then revisit the checkout page and attempt verification again.

Try a Different Device (Optional): If the issue persists, consider trying to complete your purchase with AARP discount verification from a different device (e.g., computer vs. phone). This can help identify if the issue is device-specific.

Seeking Additional Support: Contacting Kindle Customer Service

If, after trying these troubleshooting steps, you're still encountering a membership verification error, don't hesitate to contact Kindle customer service. Here's how to reach them:

Online Help Center: The Kindle store's online help center offers a wealth of information and resources. Search for "AARP discount verification error" or browse relevant sections for troubleshooting guidance.

Live Chat Support: The Kindle store offers live chat support with customer service representatives. Explain the situation clearly, mentioning the error message and any troubleshooting steps you've already tried.

Phone Support: For those who prefer phone support, contact the Kindle customer service hotline. Be prepared to provide details about the error and your AARP membership.

Additional Tips for Streamlined Verification

HOW TO GET AARP DISCOUNTS ON KINDLE EBOOK

Here are some additional tips to ensure a smooth and error-free membership verification process:

Link Your AARP Account (Optional): Some users report success by linking their AARP account directly to their Amazon account. This can potentially streamline the verification process at checkout. However, confirm if this option is available in your region before proceeding.

Maintain Updated Account Information: Ensure both your AARP membership information and your Amazon account details are current and accurate. This minimizes the possibility of mismatched information causing verification errors.

Consider Alternative Verification Methods (if available): In some cases, the Kindle store might offer alternative verification methods beyond email address or account login. Explore these options if available, as they might resolve the issue.

By understanding the reasons behind membership verification errors and employing the troubleshooting techniques outlined in this section, you're well-equipped to overcome these obstacles. Remember, a little persistence and clear communication with AARP or Kindle customer service can ensure a smooth verification process and ultimately, secure your AARP discounts on captivating eBooks. So, with this knowledge at hand, confidently navigate the checkout process and embark on your rewarding journey of literary discovery at a discount!

Addressing Discount Not Appearing at Checkout.

The excitement of discovering AARP-discounted eBooks can quickly turn into frustration when the discount fails to appear at checkout. This section equips you with the knowledge and troubleshooting steps to address this issue and ensure you secure the savings you deserve.

Understanding Discount Application: The Intricate Dance of Eligibility

The absence of an AARP discount at checkout can stem from various reasons. Here's a breakdown of the factors at play:

- **Eligibility Requirements:** AARP discounts on eBooks might have specific eligibility criteria. Ensure your chosen title qualifies for the discount program. Look for disclaimers or exclusions within the product description or on the AARP website.
- **Expired or Inactive Membership:** The most common culprit is an inactive or expired AARP membership. Double-check your membership status through your AARP account to ensure it's current and in good standing.
- **Timing Discrepancies:** Occasionally, AARP discounts might have limited time windows or promotional periods. The discount you saw on the product page might no longer be valid by the time you reach checkout.
- **Technical Glitches (Uncommon):** While less frequent, technical glitches on the Kindle store's side might cause the discount to not be reflected accurately at checkout. These are typically resolved quickly by Amazon.

Resurfacing the Discount: Strategies for Securing Savings

Here's a step-by-step approach to troubleshoot the absence of an AARP discount at checkout:

1. **Verify AARP Membership Status:** Start by logging into your AARP account and confirming your membership's active status. An expired or inactive membership will prevent the discount from being applied.
2. **Review Product Description:** Revisit the product page for the AARP-discounted eBook. Scrutinize the description to ensure the discount is still valid and hasn't expired due to a limited-time offer or promotional period.
3. **Clear Browser Cache and Cookies (Optional):** Outdated browser cache or cookies might, in rare cases, interfere with the discount application. Try clearing your browser cache and cookies, then revisit

HOW TO GET AARP DISCOUNTS ON KINDLE EBOOK

the product page and add the eBook to your cart again.
4. **Check for Alternative Offers (Optional):** If the AARP discount is no longer applicable, explore alternative discounts or promotions on the Kindle store. You might find a different offer available for the same eBook.

Seeking Additional Support: Contacting AARP or Kindle Customer Service

If, after trying these steps, the AARP discount remains absent, consider contacting either AARP or Kindle customer service for further assistance:

- **AARP Customer Support:** Contact AARP customer service directly for clarification on the specific discount program and eligibility requirements. They might be able to confirm if the discount should still be valid for your chosen title.
- **Kindle Customer Service:** Kindle customer service can investigate potential technical issues causing the discount to not be reflected at checkout. Explain the situation clearly, mentioning the specific eBook and any error messages you encountered.

Additional Tips for Ensuring Discount Visibility

Here are some additional tips to ensure AARP discounts appear accurately at checkout:

- **Stay Updated on AARP Discounts:** Regularly check the AARP website or subscribe to their newsletters to stay informed about current AARP discount offerings and any potential eligibility requirements or exclusions.
- **Consider Alternative Formats (Optional):** While the focus is on eBooks, explore if the title is available in a discounted format (e.g., audiobook) through AARP partnerships. AARP might offer alternative discounts on audiobooks through partner platforms.
- **Maintain Account Security:** Ensure the email address associated

with your AARP membership matches the one linked to your Amazon account. This minimizes the possibility of mismatched information causing discount application errors.

By understanding the reasons behind a missing AARP discount at checkout and employing the troubleshooting techniques outlined in this section, you increase your chances of securing your well-deserved savings. Remember, persistence and clear communication with AARP or Kindle customer service can be valuable tools in resolving the issue. So, with this knowledge at hand, keep exploring your literary options and confidently navigate the checkout process, ultimately enjoying the rewards of AARP-discounted eBooks!

Contacting AARP or Amazon Customer Support.

Throughout your journey of acquiring AARP-discounted eBooks, you might encounter situations requiring assistance. This section equips you with the knowledge to navigate the customer support channels of both AARP and Kindle, ensuring you receive the help you need to secure your AARP discounts and maximize your savings.

Understanding When to Contact AARP vs. Kindle Customer Service

Here's a breakdown of scenarios where contacting AARP or Kindle customer service might be beneficial:

- **AARP Membership Issues:** If you have questions about your AARP membership status, renewal process, or eligibility for AARP discount programs on eBooks, contact AARP customer service directly. They are the experts on membership-related inquiries.
- **Discount Eligibility:** For concerns regarding the specific AARP discount program applicable to a certain eBook (e.g., unsure if a new release qualifies for the discount), contacting AARP customer service can provide clarification.
- **AARP Account Issues:** Difficulties logging into your AARP account, updating membership information, or linking your AARP account to your Amazon account warrant contacting AARP

HOW TO GET AARP DISCOUNTS ON KINDLE EBOOK 77

customer service for assistance.
- **Kindle Store Checkout Issues:** If you encounter problems during checkout, such as the AARP discount not being applied or error messages appearing, contact Kindle customer service. They specialize in troubleshooting technical issues within the Kindle store.
- **General Kindle Store Inquiries:** For any questions unrelated to AARP discounts but related to the Kindle store's functionality (e.g., downloading eBooks, managing your Kindle device), contacting Kindle customer service is the recommended course of action.

Reaching Out to AARP Customer Service: Multiple Channels Available

AARP offers various ways to connect with their customer service representatives:

- **AARP Website:** Visit the AARP website (https://help.aarp.org/s/article/contact-aarp) and navigate to the "Contact Us" section. Here, you can choose from various options, including email, live chat (availability may vary), or a phone call.
- **Phone Support:** For those who prefer phone support, dial the AARP customer service hotline at 1-888-OUR-AARP (1-888-687-2277). Be prepared with your AARP membership information when calling.
- **Social Media (Optional):** While not the most efficient method for resolving complex issues, AARP maintains a social media presence. You can attempt to contact them through direct messages on platforms like Twitter, but be aware response times might be slower.

Connecting with Kindle Customer Service: Exploring Support Options

Here's how to get in touch with Kindle customer service for assistance with AARP discount-related issues:

- **Kindle Help Center:** The Kindle Help Center is a comprehensive resource for troubleshooting various issues. Search for terms like

"AARP discount error" or browse relevant sections to find solutions and answers to frequently asked questions.
- **Live Chat Support:** The Kindle store offers live chat support with customer service representatives. This can be a convenient option for real-time assistance with your AARP discount concerns.
- **Phone Support (US Only):** If you're located in the United States, you can contact Kindle customer service directly by phone at 1-888-280-4331. Explain your situation clearly, mentioning the AARP discount issue and any error messages you encountered.
- **Email Support (Limited Availability):** While less common, some users report success contacting Kindle customer service via email. However, this option might not be universally available, so consult the Kindle Help Center for the most up-to-date information.

Maximizing Your Support Experience: Tips for Effective Communication

Here are some tips to ensure a productive and efficient experience when contacting either AARP or Kindle customer service:

- **Gather Information:** Before reaching out, collect relevant details about your situation. This might include the title of the eBook in question, any error messages encountered, and your AARP membership information.
- **Clearly Explain the Issue:** When explaining your situation, be clear and concise. Briefly describe the problem you're facing with the AARP discount and what troubleshooting steps you've already tried.
- **Be Polite and Patient:** Remember, customer service representatives are there to assist you. Remain polite and patient throughout the interaction.
- **Follow Up (if necessary):** If your issue isn't resolved after the initial contact, don't hesitate to follow up with AARP or Kindle customer service. Provide any additional information that might be helpful in resolving the problem.

By understanding the appropriate channels for contacting AARP or Kindle customer service, and by employing effective communication strategies, you can ensure you receive the necessary assistance to resolve AARP discount-related issues

Chapter 8

Managing Your Kindle Library and AARP Discounts.

Viewing Purchased eBooks with AARP Discounts.

Having successfully navigated the exciting world of AARP discounts, you've secured a treasure trove of discounted eBooks. Now comes the moment of pure joy – immersing yourself in captivating stories! This section delves into the various ways you can access and enjoy your AARP-discounted reads across different devices and platforms, unlocking a universe of literary exploration.

A World of Access Options: Tailoring Your Reading Experience

The beauty of Kindle eBooks lies in their inherent flexibility. Here's a breakdown of the primary methods for accessing your AARP-discounted purchases:

- **Kindle Reading App (Free):** The Kindle reading app, available for free download on smartphones, tablets, and computers, offers a convenient and readily accessible platform for your discounted eBooks. Once installed and logged in with your Amazon account, you'll gain immediate access to your entire library, including the AARP-discounted titles you so meticulously selected.
- **Kindle E-readers:** For those seeking a dedicated and immersive reading experience, investing in a Kindle e-reader might be the ideal choice. These devices are designed specifically for reading eBooks, offering a comfortable and distraction-free environment. Transfer your purchased titles (including AARP-discounted ones) to your Kindle device via Wi-Fi or USB connection.
- **Web Browser (Limited Functionality):** While not the most optimal option, you can also access your eBooks through a web browser on your computer by visiting the "Manage Your Content and Devices" page on your Amazon account. However, functionality might be

limited compared to dedicated apps or devices. This method might be suitable for occasional reading or checking specific passages but offers a less immersive experience.

Locating Your Discounted Gems: Navigating Your eBook Library

Here's a breakdown of how to locate your AARP-discounted eBooks within your chosen access method:

- **Kindle Reading App:** Open the app and navigate to the "Your Library" section. This section displays a comprehensive list of all your purchased eBooks, with AARP-discounted titles seamlessly integrated alongside full-priced purchases. Explore filtering or sorting options based on price, genre, or acquisition date to easily locate your discounted treasures.
- **Kindle E-readers:** On your Kindle device, access the "My Library" section. Similar to the Kindle reading app, this section provides a consolidated view of your entire eBook library. Sorting and filtering options are available to help you identify your AARP-discounted reads quickly.
- **Web Browser:** Log in to your Amazon account and navigate to the "Manage Your Content and Devices" page. Under the "Content" tab, you'll find a list of all your purchased eBooks, including AARP-discounted titles.

Elevating Your Reading Journey: Exploring Features and Functionalities

Here are some features and functionalities you can explore within your chosen access method to enhance your reading experience with AARP-discounted eBooks:

- **Customization Options:** Most reading apps and devices allow you to personalize the reading experience. Adjust font size and style to find a setup that optimizes comfort and minimizes eye strain. Experiment with different options to create your perfect reading

environment.
- **Built-in Dictionaries:** Look for a built-in dictionary function within your chosen access method. This invaluable tool allows you to quickly look up unfamiliar words encountered while reading your AARP-discounted eBooks, ensuring a seamless understanding of the text.
- **Note-Taking and Highlighting:** Many apps and devices offer note-taking and highlighting capabilities. Take advantage of these features to capture important passages, make annotations, or jot down thoughts as you delve into your AARP-discounted selections. This creates a more interactive reading experience and allows you to revisit key points for future reference.
- **Whispersync Technology:** A powerful feature offered by Amazon, Whispersync technology synchronizes your reading progress across different devices. This allows you to seamlessly switch between reading on your phone, tablet, or Kindle device without ever losing your place in your AARP-discounted eBooks.

Additional Considerations: Offline Reading and Device Management

Here are some additional points to keep in mind when accessing your AARP-discounted eBooks:

- **Offline Reading:** A significant benefit of the Kindle reading app and Kindle devices is the ability to download your AARP-discounted eBooks for offline reading. This grants you the freedom to enjoy your literary treasures even when you don't have an internet connection, perfect for traveling or reading in locations with limited internet access.
- **Storage Management (for devices):** Kindle devices have limited storage capacity. If you plan to amass a large collection of AARP-discounted eBooks, consider managing your device's storage by transferring some titles to cloud storage or keeping only the ones you're actively reading on the device. This ensures optimal

performance and avoids storage overload.

- **Device Compatibility:** Ensure your chosen device (phone, tablet, computer) is compatible with the Kindle reading app or the specific Kindle device model you own. Verifying compatibility beforehand prevents frustration and allows you to seamlessly access your AARP-discounted eBooks from the get-go.

Troubleshooting Tips: When Access Issues Arise

While accessing your AARP-discounted eBooks should be a smooth process, occasional hiccups might occur. Here are some troubleshooting tips to address potential issues:

- **Check for App Updates:** Ensure you're using the latest version of the Kindle reading app on your device. Outdated versions might experience compatibility issues. Update the app through your device's app store to ensure optimal functionality.
- **Restart Your Device:** A simple device restart can often resolve minor glitches that might be preventing access to your AARP-discounted eBooks. Restart your phone, tablet, or Kindle device and attempt to access your library again.
- **Verify Wi-Fi Connection (if applicable):** If you're using the Kindle app or attempting to download eBooks for offline reading, ensure you have a stable Wi-Fi connection. An unstable connection can interrupt the download process and hinder access to your AARP-discounted titles.
- **Contact Kindle Customer Service:** If the above steps don't resolve the issue, consider contacting Kindle customer service for further assistance. Explain the problem you're encountering and provide details like error messages or specific titles you're having trouble accessing. Their representatives can offer targeted solutions to ensure you regain access to your AARP-discounted reading treasures.

With the knowledge of accessing your AARP-discounted eBooks across various platforms, combined with the troubleshooting tips to address any access issues, you're now equipped to embark on a rewarding literary adventure. So, settle into your favorite reading nook, explore the features offered by your chosen access method, and lose yourself in the captivating worlds within your AARP-discounted eBook library. Happy reading!

Downloading Discounted eBooks to Your Devices.

Having secured a collection of AARP-discounted eBooks, the next step is to seamlessly transfer them to your preferred reading devices. This section equips you with the knowledge and step-by-step instructions to download your discounted treasures, unlocking the freedom of offline reading and personalized enjoyment.

Understanding Download Options: Tailoring Access to Your Needs

The beauty of Kindle eBooks lies in their flexibility. Here's a breakdown of the primary methods for downloading your AARP-discounted purchases:

Wireless Download (Wi-Fi Required): This is the most convenient method, allowing you to download your AARP-discounted eBooks directly to your device over a Wi-Fi connection. Both the Kindle reading app and Kindle e-readers support wireless downloads.

USB Transfer (for Kindle E-readers): For users with a Kindle e-reader device and a computer with a USB port, transferring eBooks via USB cable offers another option. This method is helpful if you have a limited internet connection or prefer managing your downloads on a computer.

Sending to Kindle (Email Option): While less common, Amazon offers a "Send to Kindle" feature. You can email your AARP-discounted eBooks (in compatible formats) to a specific email address linked to your Amazon account. This email triggers the download process, making the eBook available on your registered Kindle devices.

Downloading via Wi-Fi: A Step-by-Step Guide

Here's a detailed breakdown of how to download your AARP-discounted eBooks using a Wi-Fi connection, applicable to both the Kindle reading app and Kindle e-readers:

Locate the eBook: Navigate to your "Your Library" section within the Kindle reading app or "My Library" section on your Kindle device. Locate the specific AARP-discounted eBook you want to download.

Identify the Download Option: Look for a download icon or menu option labeled "Download" or "Download to Device" next to the chosen AARP-discounted eBook title.

Initiate the Download: Tap or click on the download icon/option. The download process will commence, and a progress bar might be displayed.

Verify Download Completion: Once the download is complete, the eBook will appear in your "Downloaded" section within the Kindle reading app or your Kindle device library. You can now access and enjoy your AARP-discounted read even without an internet connection.

Transferring eBooks via USB (for Kindle E-readers):

Here's how to download your AARP-discounted eBooks using a USB cable (applicable only to Kindle e-readers):

Connect Your Device: Connect your Kindle e-reader to your computer using a compatible USB cable.

Locate the Downloaded File: On your computer, navigate to the folder containing your downloaded AARP-discounted eBook (usually in MOBI or AZW format).

Transfer the File: Drag and drop the AARP-discounted eBook file from your computer folder to the "Documents" folder on your Kindle device (as seen on your computer screen).

Eject and Disconnect: Once the transfer is complete, safely eject your Kindle device from your computer and disconnect the USB cable.

Access Your Downloaded eBook: On your Kindle e-reader, navigate to the "My Library" section. You should now see your transferred AARP-discounted eBook listed and available for reading.

Sending to Kindle (Email Option):

While less commonly used, here's a brief overview of the "Send to Kindle" email option for downloading AARP-discounted eBooks:

Locate Your Send to Kindle Email Address: Log in to your Amazon account and navigate to the "Manage Your Content and Devices" page. Under the "Preferences" section for "Send to Kindle," you'll find a unique email address assigned to your account.

Prepare the Email: From your preferred email provider, compose a new email addressed to the specific "Send to Kindle" email address.

Attach the eBook File: In the email body, attach the AARP-discounted eBook file you want to download (ensure it's in a compatible format like MOBI or AZW).

Send the Email: Once the email is addressed with the attached eBook file, send the email from your chosen email provider.

Verify Download: The download process will be triggered automatically. You'll receive a confirmation email once your AARP-discounted eBook is successfully downloaded to your registered Kindle devices.

Maximizing Storage Space: Managing Downloads on Your Devices

Kindle devices have limited storage capacity. Here are some tips for managing downloads and optimizing Space usage on your device:

Prioritize Active Reads: Focus on downloading AARP-discounted eBooks you're actively reading or plan to read soon. Leave less frequently accessed titles un-downloaded for online access when connected to Wi-Fi.

Utilize Cloud Storage (Optional): Consider using cloud storage services like Amazon Drive to store some of your AARP-discounted eBooks. This frees up space on your Kindle device while still allowing you to access them online or download them again when needed.

Delete Finished Books (Optional): Once you've finished reading an AARP-discounted eBook, consider deleting it from your device's storage to free up space for new titles. Remember, you can always download it again later if you wish to revisit it.

Troubleshooting Download Issues: Resolving Downloading Hiccups

While downloading AARP-discounted eBooks should be a smooth process, occasional hiccups might occur. Here are some troubleshooting tips:

Check Wi-Fi Connection (for Wireless Downloads): Ensure you have a stable Wi-Fi connection when downloading eBooks wirelessly. A weak or interrupted connection can cause download failures.

Verify Storage Space (for Kindle E-readers): If downloads fail on your Kindle device, check the remaining storage space. If the device is nearly full, free up space by following the tips mentioned above (e.g., deleting finished books).

Restart Device: A simple device restart can often resolve minor glitches that might be hindering downloads. Restart your phone, tablet, or Kindle device and attempt the download again.

Contact Kindle Customer Service: If the above steps don't resolve the issue, consider contacting Kindle customer service for further assistance. Explain the problem you're encountering and provide details like error messages or specific titles you're having trouble downloading. Their representatives can offer targeted solutions to ensure you can successfully download your AARP-discounted reading treasures.

By understanding the various download options, employing the step-by-step instructions, and implementing storage management strategies, you're now equipped to seamlessly transfer your AARP-discounted eBooks to your devices. This unlocks the freedom of offline reading, allowing you to delve into captivating stories regardless of internet connectivity. So, download your AARP-discounted treasures, explore the various reading features offered by your chosen device, and embark on a literary adventure that's both enriching and wallet-friendly!

Managing AARP eBook Subscriptions (if applicable)

While AARP offers a variety of benefits for its members, including discounts on various products and services, **currently, there is no official AARP-specific eBook subscription program directly integrated with Kindle.**

However, this section explores the landscape of eBook subscriptions and alternative options that might be of interest to AARP members seeking discounted access to a vast library of eBooks.

Understanding eBook Subscriptions: A World Beyond AARP

Several popular eBook subscription services offer access to a large library of eBooks for a monthly fee. Here's a breakdown of the concept:

- **Subscription Model:** These services operate on a subscription basis. You pay a monthly fee and gain access to a vast library of eBooks included in the subscription plan.
- **Selection Variety:** The selection of eBooks offered by different subscription services varies. Some focus on bestsellers and popular titles, while others offer a broader range, including genre fiction, classics, and independent authors.
- **Potential Cost Savings:** For voracious readers, eBook subscriptions can offer significant cost savings compared to buying individual eBooks at full price. However, consider your reading habits to determine if a subscription model aligns with your needs.

Exploring Alternatives: Subscription Services for AARP Members

While there's no dedicated AARP eBook subscription, here are some popular subscription services AARP members might find appealing:

- **Kindle Unlimited:** Amazon's own subscription service, Kindle

Unlimited, offers access to a vast library of eBooks, audiobooks, and magazines for a monthly fee. Explore the selection to see if it aligns with your reading preferences.
- **Scribd:** Another popular option, Scribd, offers a subscription service that includes eBooks, audiobooks, and even sheet music. Consider the variety of content formats offered by Scribd to see if it complements your reading habits.
- **Oyster:** Focused primarily on audiobooks, Oyster offers a subscription service with a curated selection of audiobooks across various genres. This might be a good option for AARP members who prefer audiobooks or enjoy a mix of both eBooks and audiobooks.

Evaluating Subscription Services: Choosing the Right Fit

Here are some key factors to consider when evaluating eBook subscription services:

- **Cost:** Compare monthly subscription fees across different services to find the most budget-friendly option for your needs.
- **Selection:** Carefully examine the eBook library offered by each service. Ensure it includes genres and authors you enjoy reading.
- **Free Trial Availability:** Many subscription services offer free trials. Take advantage of these trials to explore the platform and see if it suits your reading style before committing to a monthly fee.

AARP Membership Benefits Beyond eBooks: Exploring Additional Savings

While there might not be a dedicated AARP eBook subscription, AARP membership offers various benefits that can still help you save on eBooks:

- **AARP Discounts on Individual eBooks:** AARP occasionally negotiates discounts with publishers on specific eBooks. Keep an eye on AARP's website or communications for such offers.
- **AARP Member Discounts at Retailers:** Many retailers that sell

HOW TO GET AARP DISCOUNTS ON KINDLE EBOOK   91

eBooks offer discounts to AARP members. Explore AARP's benefits section to see if any of their partner retailers offer discounts on eBooks.

- **Library Borrowing:** Public libraries offer a vast selection of eBooks available for borrowing through their online lending platforms. Consider utilizing your local library's resources to access eBooks at no cost.

Although there currently isn't a specific AARP eBook subscription service, the knowledge of alternative subscription options, combined with exploring AARP's broader discount offerings and library resources, empowers you to continue your literary journey at a fraction of the cost. So, delve into the world of eBook subscriptions, explore AARP's member benefits, and discover a universe of discounted reading opportunities!

Chapter 9

Staying Updated on New AARP Discounts and Offers.

Subscribing to AARP Email Alerts

AARP membership unlocks a treasure trove of benefits, and staying informed about AARP-discounted eBooks is key to maximizing your savings. This section delves into the world of AARP email alerts, guiding you through the process of subscribing and highlighting the advantages of receiving timely notifications about discounted eBook opportunities.

Understanding AARP Email Alerts: A Personalized Information Stream

AARP email alerts offer a convenient and efficient way to receive updates tailored to your interests. Here's a breakdown of the concept:

- **Customization Options:** AARP allows you to personalize your email alerts by selecting the categories of information you wish to receive. This ensures you only get updates relevant to your preferences, including alerts about discounted eBooks.
- **Targeted Notifications:** Once subscribed with your preferences set, you'll receive targeted email notifications directly in your inbox. These emails might highlight newly available AARP discounts on specific eBooks, ongoing promotions on popular genres, or exclusive deals for AARP members.
- **Frequency Control:** You have control over the frequency of AARP email alerts. Choose to receive daily updates, weekly summaries, or opt for less frequent notifications based on your preference for information flow.

Subscribing to AARP Email Alerts: A Step-by-Step Guide

Here's a detailed guide on how to subscribe to AARP email alerts and ensure you receive timely notifications about discounted eBooks:

1. **Visit the AARP Website:** Navigate to the AARP website (https://www.aarp.org/).
2. **Sign Up or Log In:** If you haven't already, create a free AARP online account or log in to your existing account.
3. **Navigate to Preferences:** Once logged in, locate the "Preferences" or "Settings" section within your AARP account dashboard.
4. **Manage Email Subscriptions:** Look for a section titled "Email Subscriptions" or "Communication Preferences." This section allows you to manage the emails you receive from AARP.
5. **Select eBook Category:** Under the "Email Subscriptions" section, find the category related to "Discounts" or "Shopping." Look for a specific sub-category or checkbox option related to "Discounted eBooks" or "AARP Deals on eBooks." Select this option to ensure you receive notifications about discounted eBooks.
6. **Customize Frequency (Optional):** Some sections might offer options to control the frequency of email alerts. Choose the frequency that best suits your needs – daily, weekly, or less frequent updates.
7. **Save Your Preferences:** Once you've selected your preferred email categories and frequency (if applicable), click the "Save" or "Update" button to finalize your preferences.

Maximizing Your Benefits: Advantages of Email Alerts

Here's a breakdown of the advantages associated with subscribing to AARP email alerts for discounted eBooks:

- **Timely Notifications:** You'll be among the first to know about new AARP discounts on eBooks, allowing you to snag deals before they disappear. This ensures you don't miss out on potential savings.
- **Targeted Information:** By customizing your preferences, you'll only receive notifications about discounted eBooks relevant to your interests, saving you time and preventing irrelevant emails from cluttering your inbox.
- **Exclusive Offers:** AARP email alerts might occasionally highlight

exclusive deals and promotions available only to AARP members, giving you an additional edge when searching for discounted eBooks.
- **Stay Informed:** Regular email alerts keep you updated on the latest trends in discounted eBooks, allowing you to plan your reading list and budget for upcoming AARP deals.

Beyond Email Alerts: Exploring Additional Information Channels

While email alerts offer a convenient solution, here are some additional ways to stay informed about AARP-discounted eBooks:

- **AARP Website and Social Media:** Regularly visit the AARP website (https://www.aarp.org/) and explore their social media channels for updates on discounts and promotions.
- **AARP Magazine:** If you subscribe to the AARP magazine, keep an eye out for sections dedicated to book recommendations and potential discount offers.
- **AARP Member Benefits Section:** The AARP member benefits section on their website might list partnerships or ongoing promotions with eBook retailers offering AARP member discounts.

By subscribing to AARP email alerts tailored to discounted eBooks, paired with exploring additional information channels, you'll be well-equipped to discover a world of literary treasures at a fraction of the cost. So, personalize your email preferences, stay informed about upcoming deals, and embark on a rewarding journey of discounted reading adventures!

e key factors to consider when evaluating eBook subscription services:

- **Cost:** Compare monthly subscription fees across different services to find the most budget-friendly option for your needs.
- **Selection:** Carefully examine the eBook library offered by each service. Ensure it includes genres and authors you enjoy reading.
- **Free Trial Availability:** Many subscription services offer free trials. Take advantage of these trials to explore the platform and see if it suits your reading style before committing to a monthly fee.

AARP Membership Benefits Beyond eBooks: Exploring Additional Savings

While there might not be a dedicated AARP eBook subscription, AARP membership offers various benefits that can still help you save on eBooks:

- **AARP Discounts on Individual eBooks:** AARP occasionally negotiates discounts with publishers on specific eBooks. Keep an eye on AARP's website or communications for such offers.
- **AARP Member Discounts at Retailers:** Many retailers that sell eBooks offer discounts to AARP members. Explore AARP's benefits section to see if any of their partner retailers offer discounts on eBooks.
- **Library Borrowing:** Public libraries offer a vast selection of eBooks available for borrowing through their online lending platforms. Consider utilizing your local library's resources to access eBooks at no cost.

Conclusion: A World of Reading Possibilities

Although there currently isn't a specific AARP eBook subscription service, the knowledge of alternative subscription options, combined with exploring AARP's broader discount offerings and library resources, empowers you to continue your literary journey at a fraction of the cost. So, delve into the world of eBook subscriptions, explore AARP's member benefits, and discover a universe of discounted reading opportunities!

Following AARP Social Media Accounts.

In today's digital age, social media platforms have become powerful tools for staying informed and connected. This section explores how following AARP's social media accounts can be a valuable strategy for maximizing your access to AARP discounts on Kindle eBooks. Here, we'll delve into the benefits of following AARP on social media and explore specific platforms to navigate for the latest deals and announcements.

The Power of Social Media: A Stream of Discounted Discoveries

Social media platforms offer a dynamic and interactive way to connect with AARP and fellow members. Here's a breakdown of the advantages of following AARP on social media:

- **Real-Time Updates:** Social media platforms provide a constant stream of updates. By following AARP, you'll receive real-time notifications about newly available discounts, flash sales, and ongoing promotions on Kindle eBooks.
- **Engaging Content:** AARP's social media pages often feature engaging content like author interviews, book reviews, and genre-specific recommendations. This content can introduce you to new authors and discounted titles you might not have discovered otherwise.
- **Community Interaction:** Social media fosters a sense of community. Join AARP groups or discussions to connect with other members who share your passion for reading. You can exchange recommendations for discounted eBooks and discover hidden gems within the AARP discount program.
- **Interactive Features:** Many social media platforms offer interactive

features like polls and Q&A sessions. Participate in these activities to directly engage with AARP and potentially influence the types of discounted eBooks they highlight.

Navigating the Social Media Landscape: Key Platforms to Follow

Here's a breakdown of some key social media platforms to follow AARP on and how each platform can be leveraged to find discounted Kindle eBooks:

- **Facebook:** A widely used platform, Facebook offers a central hub for AARP's social media presence. "Like" the official AARP Facebook page to receive updates on their news feed, including announcements about discounted eBooks. Explore AARP groups dedicated to books or specific genres to connect with like-minded readers and discover discount recommendations.
- **Twitter:** Known for its fast-paced nature, follow AARP on Twitter (@AARP) to stay updated with the latest news and announcements. AARP might use Twitter to announce flash sales or limited-time discounts on Kindle eBooks. Utilize relevant hashtags like #aarpreads or #discountkindlebooks to discover tweets from AARP and other users sharing discounted book recommendations.
- **Instagram:** AARP's Instagram account (@aarp) offers a visually engaging platform. Follow them to see eye-catching posts featuring book covers, author spotlights, and promotions on discounted Kindle eBooks. Explore Instagram Stories for glimpses into upcoming deals or behind-the-scenes content related to AARP discounts.
- **YouTube:** While not the primary platform for discount announcements, AARP's YouTube channel (@AARP) might feature videos with author interviews or book recommendations that mention AARP discounts on Kindle eBooks. Subscribe to their channel and explore playlists related to books or literature to discover relevant content.

Engaging with AARP on Social Media: Maximizing the Benefits

Here are some tips for maximizing your experience while following AARP on social media:

- **Turn on Notifications:** Enable notifications for AARP's social media posts to ensure you don't miss important updates about discounted eBooks.
- **Participate in Discussions:** Join conversations on AARP's social media pages by commenting, sharing, and asking questions. This increases your chances of discovering hidden gems and recommendations from the AARP community.
- **Utilize Search Functions:** Each social media platform has a search function. Use relevant keywords like "AARP discount," "Kindle books," or specific genres to find past posts or discussions about discounted eBooks.
- **Follow Relevant Hashtags:** Follow hashtags frequently used by AARP and the book community, such as #aarpreads or #discountkindlebooks. This exposes you to a wider range of content related to discounted eBooks.

Beyond Social Media: Exploring Additional Resources

While social media offers valuable insights, here are some additional resources to consider for finding AARP discounts on Kindle eBooks:

- **AARP Website:** The AARP website (https://www.aarp.org/) is a wealth of information. Explore sections dedicated to shopping and discounts to see if there are current promotions on Kindle eBooks.
- **AARP Email Alerts:** Signing up for AARP email alerts tailored to "Discounts" or "Shopping" can notify you directly about new deals on Kindle eBooks.
- **AARP Magazine:** The AARP magazine might feature articles or advertisements highlighting discounted eBooks available through AARP partnerships.

By strategically following AARP's social media accounts and engaging with the online community, you'll transform yourself from a passive reader to a social media-savvy discount hunter. You'll gain access to a real-time stream of information, discover hidden gems through community recommendations, and potentially influence the types of content AARP highlights. So, follow AARP on your preferred social media platforms, turn on notifications, participate in discussions, and leverage the power of social media to unlock a world of discounted literary treasures on your Kindle device!

The AARP website serves as your central hub for accessing information and maximizing the benefits of your membership. This section delves into the AARP website as a valuable tool for discovering ongoing deals on Kindle eBooks. We'll explore key sections, functionalities, and search strategies to help you unearth a universe of discounted reading material.

Understanding the AARP Website Layout: A Roadmap to Discounted Delights

The AARP website offers a user-friendly interface with various sections dedicated to different aspects of membership benefits. Here's a breakdown of key areas to explore for finding AARP discounts on Kindle eBooks:

- **Membership Section:** Once logged in, access the "Membership" section. This section might provide an overview of current benefits and promotions, potentially including discounts on Kindle eBooks.
- **Benefits Section:** Navigate to the "Benefits" section. This area showcases various discounts and deals available to AARP members. Explore categories like "Shopping" or "Entertainment" to see if there are ongoing promotions with Kindle or eBook retailers.
- **Search Function:** The AARP website offers a powerful search function. Utilize keywords like "Kindle eBooks," "discounted eBooks," or specific genres to find relevant information about AARP discounts and partner programs.

HOW TO GET AARP DISCOUNTS ON KINDLE EBOOK

Exploring Specific Pages: Unveiling Discount Opportunities

Here's a deeper dive into some specific pages within the AARP website that might hold the key to discounted Kindle eBooks:

- **AARP Shopping Page:** Visit the "Shopping" page on the AARP website. This page often features deals and promotions from partner retailers, and some might offer discounts on Kindle eBooks. Look for logos of known eBook retailers or browse through current shopping offers.
- **AARP Travel Page (Optional):** While seemingly unrelated, the AARP Travel page might occasionally partner with travel publishers or retailers offering discounted travel eBooks. If travel literature is your genre of choice, explore this section for potential deals.
- **AARP Book Recommendations:** AARP's website might feature sections dedicated to book recommendations or reviews. These sections might highlight discounted eBooks available through AARP partnerships or mention deals offered by specific publishers.

Mastering Search Strategies: Unearthing Hidden Gems

Here are some effective search strategies to maximize your chances of finding AARP discounts on Kindle eBooks:

- **Keyword Refinement:** Refine your search terms beyond just "Kindle eBooks." Include specific genres you enjoy (e.g., "mystery discount ebooks aarp") or the names of publishers known for offering AARP discounts.
- **Utilize Filters (if available):** If the search function offers filters, utilize them to narrow down your results. For example, filter by "Discounts" or "Shopping" to focus on deal-oriented content.
- **Explore Past Deals (if applicable):** Some websites allow searching past content. If available, try searching for past articles or announcements related to "AARP Kindle discounts" to discover trends and potential ongoing promotions.

Staying Updated: Utilizing Additional Website Features

Beyond actively searching, here are some additional website features to leverage for staying informed about AARP discounts on Kindle eBooks:

- **AARP Email Alerts:** Sign up for AARP email alerts tailored to "Discounts" or "Shopping." These alerts can notify you directly about new deals on Kindle eBooks.
- **AARP Blog:** The AARP website might have a blog section featuring articles on various topics. Explore the blog and search for articles mentioning "Kindle eBooks" or "discounted books" to discover potential deals.
- **AARP Social Media Links:** The AARP website might provide links to their social media accounts. Follow these links to connect with AARP on social media platforms and gain access to real-time updates about ongoing discounts (further explored in a separate section of this guide).

Complementary Resources: Expanding Your Discounting Reach

While the AARP website offers a wealth of information, consider these complementary resources for a more comprehensive approach to finding discounted Kindle eBooks:

- **Kindle Daily Deals:** Check the "Daily Deals" section on the Kindle website (https://www.amazon.com/amz-books/book-deals) or app. Every day, Amazon offers limited-time discounts on various products, including eBooks. Keep an eye out for discounted titles that align with your interests.
- **Publisher Websites:** Many publishers offer discounts directly through their websites. Explore the websites of your favorite publishers or those known for offering AARP discounts to see if they have any ongoing promotions.
- **eBook Discount Websites:** Several websites specialize in aggregating eBook deals from various retailers. Explore these websites to find

discounted Kindle eBooks beyond just AARP-specific promotions.

Conclusion: A Website Well-Navigated: Unlocking a World of Discounted Reads

By understanding the AARP website's layout, exploring dedicated pages, employing effective search strategies, and utilizing complementary resources, you'll transform yourself from a casual website visitor into a discount-savvy navigator. You'll unearth a universe of discounted Kindle eBooks, maximizing the value of your AARP membership and enriching your reading life without breaking the bank. So, log in to the AARP website, refine your search skills, leverage email alerts, and explore the world of discounted eBooks waiting to be discovered! Remember, a little exploration goes a long way in unlocking a treasure trove of literary delights at a fraction of the cost. Happy reading!

www.ingramcontent.com/pod-product-compliance
Lightning Source LLC
Chambersburg PA
CBHW071835210526
45479CB00001B/150